FLOWERS
FOR THE HOME

MALCOLM HILLIER

PHOTOGRAPHY BY STEPHEN HAYWARD

A Dorling Kindersley Book

LONDON, NEW YORK, MUNICH, MELBOURNE, DELHI

Editors • *May Corfield, Jennifer Lane*

Design Direction • *Mason Linklater*

Managing Editor • *Gillian Roberts*

Senior Art Editor • *Karen Sawyer*

Category Publisher • *Mary-Clare Jerram*

DTP Designers • *Sonia Charbonnier, Louise Waller*

Production Controller • *Joanna Bull*

First published in Great Britain in 2000
by Dorling Kindersley Limited

This edition published in Great Britain in 2003
by Dorling Kindersley Limited
80 Strand, London WC2R 0RL
A Penguin Company

A CIP catalogue record for this book is available
from The British Library

ISBN 0 7513 4640 3

Colour reproduced by GRB Editrice Srl, Italy
Printed and bound by MOHN media and
Mohndruck GmbH, Germany

See our complete catalogue at
www.dk.com

CONTENTS

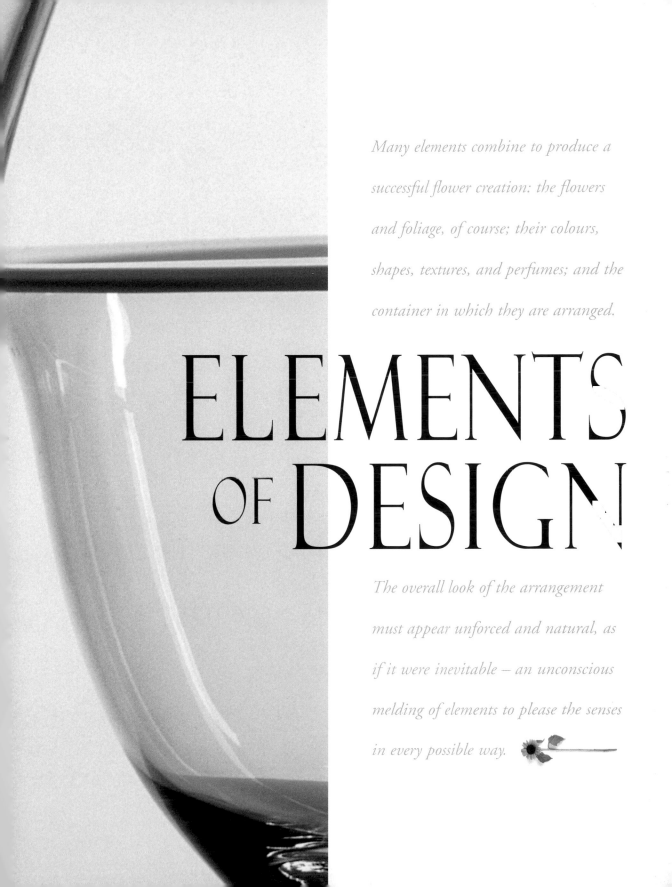

Many elements combine to produce a successful flower creation: the flowers and foliage, of course; their colours, shapes, textures, and perfumes; and the container in which they are arranged.

ELEMENTS OF DESIGN

The overall look of the arrangement must appear unforced and natural, as if it were inevitable – an unconscious melding of elements to please the senses in every possible way.

Colour

Of all the attributes we notice in flowers, colour is perhaps the most immediate. It invariably creates the most powerful visual impact, while the choice of particular colours can generate a range of different emotional responses. To understand just how colour produces such different effects and moods, we need to understand a little about colour theory and how colours relate to one another. This relationship is commonly explained using a colour wheel (*right*), which is composed of primary, secondary, and tertiary colours.

Primary colours

Red, blue, and yellow are the three primary colours: they cannot be created by mixing other colours. All the colours in the spectrum, however, can be produced by combining the primaries and adding black or white. Secondary colours are created by mixing two of the primary colours. In the colour wheel each secondary lies opposite the third unmixed primary.

secondary

tertiary

tertiary

primary

tertiary

secondary

Red

Yellow

Blue

SECONDARIES

Green, orange, and violet are the three secondary colours of the colour wheel and are produced by mixing two primaries together: blue and yellow to make green, red and yellow for orange, and red and blue for violet. Colours that lie opposite each other on the colour wheel – for example, primary yellow and secondary violet, or primary blue and secondary orange – are known as complementary colours and actually enhance one another when they are placed side by side. These combinations can create stunning visual effects.

primary

tertiary

secondary

tertiary

primary

tertiary

Orange

Green

Violet

TERTIARIES

Turquoise, indigo, purple, scarlet, gold, and lime-green are tertiary colours and are made by mixing various combinations of primaries and secondaries that lie adjacent to one another on the colour wheel. Blue and green make turquoise, violet and blue make indigo, red and yellow together make gold, and green and yellow combined make lime-green. On the right-hand side of the colour wheel are the warmer colours; on the left, the cooler hues. By adding white, which creates lighter hues, or black, which deepens a colour, a variety of paler or darker versions of all these colours can be produced.

Turquoise

Indigo

Purple

Scarlet

Gold

Lime-green

PROPERTIES OF COLOUR

Understanding the particular characteristics of any colour ensures that the most appropriate flowers can be used in an arrangement to harmonize the piece and create the right style and mood. Whether saturated or pale, intense or tinted, certain colours can be used effectively to create either an elegant or a rustic effect or a vibrant or demure look.

Passionate red

The hottest and most concentrated of colours in the spectrum, red is extremely vibrant and instantly eye-catching. Red evokes powerful emotions, symbolizing love and passion but also confusion and danger. It can be a warm and positive colour, yet also provocative and angry.

Mellow yellow

The closest of colours to white, yellow is therefore also the brightest. Clean and fresh, it induces feelings of happiness and security. It is also a warm colour, evocative of spring and summer. Its clarity and radiance make it seem to leap out at the eye. It is the easiest of colours to use and mixes well in arrangements.

Tranquil blue

Pure blue is a cool colour that is a fairly uncommon hue in a flower; most blue flowers lean towards the red or green end of the spectrum. Blue evokes tranquillity and creates a feeling of space and height, but can also look muted and drab when mixed with intense colours such as red.

Fiery orange

Orange is a warm colour, the colour of autumn and the dying embers of a fire. The brightest of oranges are sunny and welcoming; the deeper hues have a wistful quality that does not bring out the best in other colours, especially purple and violet.

Serene green

Green is the most serene of colours. It is cooling and calming, gentle and refreshing, and the natural opposite of red on the colour wheel. It is the most constant colour in flower arranging and fortunately complements all other hues.

Demure violet

Violet lies at the dark, moody end of the spectrum. It is an enigmatic colour, demure and withdrawn yet carrying an intense, secretive beauty. It harmonizes well with adjacent colours, but really only shines and radiates when paired with yellow.

COMPLEMENTARY COLOURS

Mixing colours is always an exciting process. For sheer vibrancy that almost takes the breath away, those colours that lie opposite one another on the spectrum are the ones that create the most stunning effects. Contrasting opposites occur between a primary and a secondary colour such as red and green, or two tertiaries, such as lime-green and purple. Such bold contrasts in colour will enliven a look still further. This is particularly true when a small amount of one colour is mixed with a large quantity of its complementary opposite. The small selection of colour seems to become even more intense, so creating a greater impact.

Red and green

The fiery heat of red shades set against the cool, refreshingly restful hues of green make this an immensely exciting pair of complementary colours. It is a combination that occurs naturally in the garden, where the green foliage of the plants immediately offsets any flush of red blooms.

Blue and orange

Perhaps the most vibrant colour opposites of all are primary blue and secondary orange. Although true blue hues are rarely found in flowers, with many so-called blue flowers actually betraying hints of lilac and mauve, it is the cooler notes of blue, when contrasted with the sunny sharpness of orange, that cause a blue flower to become so intense and lively. Likewise, the startling brightness of orange becomes even more luscious if set against a mass of blue flowers.

Yellow and violet

Primary yellow is the most joyous colour of the spectrum and it marks the start of the warm half of the colour wheel; by contrast, violet is a more sombre, subtle colour. When mixed together, however, the extraordinarily luminous concentration of yellow flowers becomes even brighter than before, while the interludes of deep violet shades seem to almost vibrate in intensity. Lime-green foliage and blooms will also create a visually stunning impact when set against deep pinks, violets, and purples.

Contrasting opposites: red & green

Contrasting opposites: blue & orange

Contrasting opposites: violet & yellow

HARMONIES AND GENTLE CONTRASTS

A harmonious relationship between colours is usually determined by the order and proportion of colours used. The most successful combinations of harmonious colours are those that lie close to one another on the colour spectrum and which combine to create an effect that is pleasing and easy on the eye. As the colour pairings move further apart on the colour wheel, so the contrasts become greater. The range of mixes can also be complicated by the ubiquitous presence of green, and/or the degree of lightness or darkness of a particular hue.

Adjacent harmonies

Those hues that lie adjacent to one another on the colour wheel are comparatively easy to harmonize and unify. For instance, scarlet, a tertiary, combined with either red or orange which lie on either side of scarlet, will produce a richly satisfying blend of saturated, harmonized colour. Though these hues appear to be uniformly intense, they combine together with an assured ease that is visually satisfying, and likewise with such combinations as orange and yellow, yellow and green, turquoise and blue, and so on.

Primary contrasts: red & blue

Gentle contrasts: lime-green & peach

Close contrasts: scarlet & purple

Gentle contrasts

Those colours that lie close, though not adjacent, to each other on the colour wheel will generate a series of gentle contrasts. When combined, they create a heightened visual effect while still harmonizing. This is particularly true if these gentle contrasts cross the border between the hotter and cooler ends of the spectrum, either side of warm lime-green and cool purple. The correct proportion and mix of colours will heighten the concentration of each flower with subtle vibrancy.

Moderate contrasts

Creating a look that enhances the visual impact of a flower arrangement without producing a startling result can be achieved by combining colours that lie up to three or four positions apart on the colour wheel. This mix of colours will usually include any two of the three primary colours. Such a combination of yellow with blue, red with blue, or red with yellow, can create strong effects. Include paler or darker secondaries and tertiaries, such as pale pink and peach, if you want to tone down the impact.

Close harmonies: orange & yellow

Medium contrasts: purple & green

Close harmonies: orange, cream, & yellow

CHANGING BACKGROUNDS

There are no hard and fast rules for choosing which colours will best complement each other, but there are general guidelines to achieving the most interesting and dynamic effects. To illustrate the way in which different colours interact to produce different effects, this harmonious arrangement of yellow, cream, and green poppies, eustoma, and golden rod in a simple glass vase has been pictured against five differently coloured backgrounds, and demonstrates dramatically the power and influence of colour.

BLUE, a primary colour, shows up yellow (another primary) surprisingly well. The flowers stand out bright and fresh against this background; the green foliage, which is closer to blue, becomes muted.

GREEN is considered a harmonizing colour. A deeper green would have made the flowers stand out and the foliage almost disappear; here the richer golden yellow flowers still create impact against this lighter shade.

YELLOW is a strong colour that can detract from more muted hues. While easy on the eye, the effect of this yellow background on the flowers is such that they lose all definition and almost vanish.

NEUTRAL, with its off-white hue, is close to yellow in tone but since it is so pale it harmonizes well with the flowers while still showing them off. The pale green leaves begin to merge gently with the neutral wall.

RED, with its rich, dark hues, makes both the flowers and foliage of this arrangement stand out dramatically. Here are complementary green and red at their most effective, while the yellow blooms glow luminously.

JUXTAPOSING COLOURS

Any two colours placed together will have an immediate effect on each other, and any harmonization or contrast between the two will immediately be accentuated. Here, the same arrangement of rich purple and violet anemones, burgundy ranunculus, and purple liatris in a glass container have been set against the same five coloured backgrounds as on the previous pages. The effects created by this display, however, are dramatically different from those of the previous yellow, cream, and green arrangement.

BLUE is relatively close to purple and violet on the colour wheel. As a result the flowers in the vase harmonize with the blue background, so losing their individual strength and clarity.

GREEN lies far enough from purple on the colour wheel to provide an effective contrast to these flowers. This makes the blooms seem more saturated, while the foliage of the anemones appears to recede.

RED is closely associated with many of the purples and violets in this arrangement. The anemones in particular almost disappear into the background, while the green foliage leaps out of the picture.

NEUTRAL shades are perfect for showing off these rich colours as they create an effective contrast to both flowers and foliage. The lightness of the background makes the flowers look larger and brighter.

YELLOW is the direct opposite of violet on the colour wheel and so provides the most effective contrast for these flowers. This wall of yellow makes the arrangement appear at its strongest and richest.

CONTAINER SHAPES

THE SHAPE OF a container is a crucial factor in any flower arrangement. Having a selection of vessels to choose from makes an enormous difference to the quantity, size, and type of flowers and foliage that you will be able to select and buy. Bear in mind that the style and diameter of the neck of the container will have a marked influence on the overall shape of the final arrangement. Aside from the question of shape, the colour and any decorative qualities on the exterior of a container are also worth considering.

fluted trumpet vase

large rectangular vase

rounded "goldfish"

urn-shaped pedestal

small round vase

SELECTION OF SHAPES

There is now an enormous range of different container shapes available on the market – from a low, shallow bowl to a tall cylinder, from a classical urn shape to a tazza, from a goldfish bowl to a trumpet vase – all of them produced in an increasingly inventive and interesting array of materials. It is certainly true that some container shapes are much better for arranging flowers than others: any container that holds stems in place satisfactorily will make the task of placing flowers in an attractive and pleasing way much easier. Trumpet and cylindrical shapes are among the most effective containers in which to arrange flowers and foliage, because both the rims and the edges at the bottom of these vases will hold the ingredients securely in place, like pencils in a mug. The rounded shape of a goldfish-bowl-shaped container is more difficult to work with, particularly when the flower heads are heavy. When this is the case, the stems will tend to rise up to the widest part of the bowl and can easily lift up out of their water as a result. Narrow-topped vases, on the other hand, automatically

tall cylindrical vase

narrow-necked vase

large tazza

small square vase

narrow-waisted vase

restrict the amount of stems and foliage that can be placed in them, but this factor can also be beneficial if you do not wish to buy too much material for your arrangement.

Low, shallow bowls that curve outwards, wide cylindrical or rectangular vases, and tazzas are not easy containers to arrange flowers and foliage in, unless you simply float flower heads on the surface of the water. If you do decide to use such containers for arranging flowers, the first stems at least will usually need to have some form of support. Foam, pinholder, marbles, or wire mesh are all possibilities. If the bowl or vase is made of clear glass and you use foam as a support, you will have to devise a means of hiding it – for example by putting a layer of green moss against the inner edges, which can then be held in place by the foam.

If you wish to select just four basic vases for everyday flower arrangements at home, I suggest that you choose a cylindrical vase 23cm (9in) tall, a narrow rectangular vase measuring 20 x 20 x 8cm (8 x 8 x 3in), a trumpet-shaped vase approximately 18cm (7in) tall, and a round bowl in which to float flower heads.

DISPLAY SHAPES

THERE ARE NO HARD AND FAST RULES concerning the shape of an arrangement and, so long as the display doesn't look top-heavy or precariously balanced, any shape that looks comfortable in its setting should be fine. There are, however, several factors to consider when planning the eventual look. The scale of the arrangement should be in keeping with the size of the setting and, in general, the flowers should not be more than twice the height of the vase. Consider whether the arrangement will suit a formal or casual setting, for instance, and ensure that it does not block anyone's path or restrict their view at a dining table.

THE THREE-DIMENSIONAL ASPECT

A flower arrangement should always look complete and balanced in its setting. While this doesn't mean that a display must always look as finished at the back as at the front (which would also increase the cost and amount of plant materials), it does mean that the arrangement should look good at every angle from which it can be seen. It should also give the impression that the back of the arrangement would look as good as the front if it was on view.

Giving the display a three-dimensional effect usually achieves this, even if the display is going to sit flush against a wall. Arrange the flowers so that they don't just face to the front, but lean back, up, and out to the sides to achieve a rounded effect. Ensure that arrangements are positioned comfortably in a container to ensure the right balance – and do check that any foam, wires, chicken wire, or tube extensions are concealed.

Curved display
The most common shape in flower arranging is one that creates a rounded, fan-shaped effect rising from a container. Depending on the particular situation and setting, this can be a front-facing or all-round display and its size can be as variable as the selection of flowers you choose. Aim for soft, broken curves and natural groupings of moderately contrasting flowers and colours.

Triangular display
Triangular-shaped arrangements can vary from a low, flattened, three-pointed display such as the one above (which would be particularly suitable as an all-round centrepiece for a dining table) to a tall, front-facing triangular arrangement that will also look effective when viewed from the side. This type of arrangement is more complicated to achieve successfully than a curved display.

Conical display

The diameter of the mouth of a vase is a determining factor in the final shape of an arrangement; a conical vase, which is a good container for easy arranging, creates a very attractive shape for flowers and foliage. To achieve a conical effect, give the display a good height by ensuring the flowers are at least twice as high as the vase. This shape is good for all-round and front-facing displays.

Asymmetrical display

A tilted, triangular shape can work well, particularly if the stems are also visible through the transparent sides of a rectangular glass vase. This type of display works best if it is one-dimensional, so ensure that the front-to-back depth of the vase is narrow enough to hold the display securely. This arrangement is just one flower deep, but it looks equally beautiful from the front and the back.

Low all-round display

An arrangement that is ideal for table centres and coffee tables, this display has as its base a ring of foam that ensures the flowers can be arranged into a compact, almost flat, low mound shape. As these arrangements are mostly seen from above they need to look good from every angle and should be evenly arranged. To maintain the impact of this display, keep the plant materials simple.

Rectangular display

The effect of this arrangement is similar to that of a window box of flowers, so it is best to use a long box-shaped container. The flowers are arranged so that they stand upright, imitating growing plants. This type of arrangement works best if it is created as a three-sided display with just the suggestion of a back, and then positioned against a wall, mirror, or on a shelf.

TEXTURE

TEXTURE IS A SENSUAL as well as a visual element of flower arranging. The appearance and feel of various plant materials, such as leaves and petals, bark and moss, stems and seed heads, combined with the textural surface of a container, become major elements in the make-up of a flower display. Being aware of the possibilities of combining textures can add an extra dimension to every arrangement.

TEXTURED CONTAINERS

Whether it is the uneven texture of roughly woven twigs or wicker, or the smooth, cool, silky surface quality of glass, the texture of a container will influence and accentuate the overall look of an arrangement. Wicker, bark, and rough terracotta containers work particularly well with seed heads, pine cones, and any dried plant materials. Yet such rough textures also work effectively when they are juxtaposed with the waxy smoothness of orchids, for example, or the velvety petals of peonies. Mixing and matching such a wide variety of textures ensures that you will produce more sensual creations.

Brass and copper
Although brass and copper both have smooth surfaces, any interesting burnished and tarnished areas can easily be seen and felt. Such materials work well with autumn colours and dried flowers.

Glass
Sometimes silky smooth, sometimes like wax, glass also looks effective when it is roughly etched like chipped ice. This material makes for one of the best containers for fresh flower arrangements.

Woven raffia
Raffia, which is made from the stalks of the palm Raphia, has a crinkly texture that is accentuated when it is woven. Use it as ties for bouquets or woven into baskets for a natural look and feel.

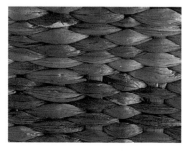

Galvanized steel
This material has a crystalline surface texture that improves with age. The flower-bucket shape of most galvanized steel containers is perfect for large and small fresh flower arrangements.

Terracotta
With its warm tones, rough texture, and pitted surface, terracotta is a popular choice. Although it is a porous material, terracotta will serve very well if the container is first lined with plastic.

Woven twigs
Layering texture upon texture, each twig in a woven basket has a rough grain running through the surface of its woody stem. The shape of the basket often serves to accentuate these textures.

COMBINING TEXTURES

A flower arrangement will become more fascinating and exciting if unusual combinations of textures are incorporated to create a visually stimulating display. Try taking the textures of rough and smooth to extremes: combine delicate but brittle shells with creamy flower bouquets, velvety petals with the hard coldness of marble, or twigs and pine cones with patinated bronze. Every flower will also have its own textures, such as the seed capsules of sunflowers, the fragile throats of orchids, the rich, sumptuous softness of rose and peony petals, the rough quality of sage leaves, or the spiky notes of butcher's broom.

Similar textures

The ruff of silky textured deep red feathers looks wonderful when mixed with rich, velvety crimson peonies in this wedding bouquet, making it sensuous to touch and beautiful to behold.

Contrasting textures

A polished satin-finished steel pot filled with a brush of chopped papyrus leaves creates a spiky crown effect across the immaculately smooth, domed ball. Little waxy berries add textural detail.

Complementary textures

This basket made from plaited palm leaves has a similar texture to the fleshy leaves of the artichoke flower. Both the poppy heads and the sea holly echo this tactile textural pattern.

We all need some inspiration, and the wealth of arrangements in these pages will act as a catalyst to help in your own creations. Here, you will find ideas to fill your living room, hallway, bedroom, or even kitchen with colour,

INSPIRATIONS

texture, and scent, as well as special celebration flowers for dinner parties or creations for al fresco entertaining in the garden. Seasonal availability, longevity, and level of difficulty is shown for each project.

✳ availability of ingredients   ✳ longevity of display

✳✳ level of difficulty

VALENTINE HEARTS

IT SEEMS ALMOST mandatory to use the heart-shaped flowers and leaves of anthuriums in a Valentine's day arrangement. Here, I have used a clear glass vase to display the rich pink spathes of *Anthurium andraeanum 'Lunette'* and the dark green leaves of *Anthurium crystallinum* and *Colocasia esculenta*.

Ingredients

Colocasia esculenta

Anthurium andraeanum 'Lunette'

Anthurium crystallinum

Alternative with *red*

While I would say that pink anthuriums are more beautiful than the red, it is undeniable that red has become the colour most associated with Valentine's day. For those people who are sticklers for tradition, here is the red version, for which I have used *Anthurium andraeanum* 'Tropical' with its deep red spathes and green spadices. The display looks good on a glass, stone, or pale wood surface, or even standing against a mirror.

DISPLAYING THE HEARTS

• Cut one leaf of *Anthurium crystallinum* and one spathe of *Anthurium andraeanum 'Lunette'* and submerge them in the water-filled glass vase. They will not last as long under the water as above, but it is fun to arrange them like this, and they will look fine in the water for three or four days.

• Take the large green leaf of *Colocasia esculenta* and twirl its tip into the mouth of the vase. The stem pokes down into the water at the back of the arrangement.

• Arrange the heart-shaped flowers and leaves above the water in a loose, asymmetrical style. The spathes have a tendency to settle upside down – the plant world has no concept of Valentine's day.

• Remove the submerged leaf and spathe after three or four days, and substitute clean water. The display above the water will last for another ten days or so.

SPRING YELLOWS

THIS EXOTIC APPROACH to spring colour uses calla lilies (*Zantedeschia*) and dramatic crown imperials (*Fritillaria*), alongside stocks (*Matthiola*), day jessamine (*Cestrum*), and sandersonia, a delicate South African flower that blooms in summer but is available throughout the year from florists. The combination makes a modern arrangement that is ideal for a side table.

Alternative with *quince*

The addition of a few twigs of red-flowered ornamental quince (*Chaenomeles*), creates quite a different colour emphasis. Although only a small amount of red is added, the whole arrangement seems much warmer. It is always worth experimenting with combinations – the results are often a pleasant surprise.

PREPARE THE MATERIAL

• Remove all the lower leaves of the crown imperials; they rot very quickly once they are submerged in water.

• If possible, change the water of this arrangement every day: the stems of both the stocks and the crown imperials rot easily. Always use a few drops of bleach or some flower food in the water to help keep harmful bacteria at bay.

• This arrangement is best placed some distance from any seating area, as the smell of the crown imperials is slightly unpleasant, but not enough to warrant excluding them from displays.

Ingredients

Fritillaria imperialis

Zantedeschia 'Aztec Gold'

Sandersonia aurantiaca

Cestrum diurnum

Matthiola incana

LENTEN ROSES

THE BEAUTIFUL NODDING flowers of Lenten roses (*Helleborus orientalis*) enliven the dark days at the close of winter. The garden hybrids look wonderful outdoors, but their amazing colours and spotted markings are best appreciated when facing upwards and floating in a shiny bowl. With their stems cut short, they will give pleasure for a week.

USING HELLEBORES

• Hellebores are available in an enormous range of colours: my favourite is intense green. All flower from the middle of winter to the middle of spring.

• Neither the Lenten rose nor the other related hellebores, such as the Christmas rose (*Helleborus niger*), will last well if the flowers are left on the full stems. Before arranging them in lukewarm water, pierce each stem with a pin a few times just below the heads; this may give them a life of three or four days.

• It is best to cut the stems really short – to no more than 1cm (½in) – and float the flowers on water, as in this arrangement; then they should last for a week.

• Remember that all parts of the hellebore are mildly toxic and the sap that bleeds from the stems can irritate skin.

• Hellebores are very variable, and there are many different cultivars and hybrids. Those shown here are from my garden. If you too want to grow hellebores, try to view them in flower at a specialist nursery before buying.

Ingredients

Helleborus orientalis hybrid

Helleborus orientalis hybrid

Helleborus orientalis hybrid

Helleborus orientalis hybrid

Alternative with *hyacinths and forsythia*

The main arrangement is elegant and restrained, in shades from cream to purple. A fresher feel can be achieved by adding other spring colours. Here, single flowers cut from a pale Delft-blue hyacinth and a stem of sunny yellow forsythia replace some of the deeper-toned Lenten roses. Another alternative would be to include white or pink camellias, whose waxy blooms resemble those of floating water lilies.

CREATIVE WRAPS

INSPIRED BY Japanese presentation skills, this
idea involves simply wrapping up vases so that
the paper forms a ruff around the flowers. I
think the best result is achieved with plain white
textured paper, perhaps with some plant material
woven into it, but you can use any type, from
silky tissue or textured, handmade paper bound
with ribbon, to crisp brown wrapping paper tied
with string. These very easy creations are perfect
for a lunch or dinner party, with single flowers
in shot glasses at each place setting and a larger
arrangement for the centre of the table.

Ingredients

Rosa 'Candy Bernice'

Rosa 'Hollywood'

Rosa 'Golden Gate'

WRAPPING THE GLASSES

- The best shot glasses for this form of presentation are those with thick, heavy bases, as they are the most stable.
- Choose paper to match both the look of the flowers and the scale of the glass; small glasses are easier to wrap in soft papers.
- Cut or tear the wrapping paper into squares, making each side of the square about four times the height of the glass. Torn edges generally look best.

Alternative with *light*

To create a whole table setting, make a lamp by wrapping a goldfish bowl holding a nightlight in the same paper used on the glasses. Tie the cord or ribbon just below the rim of the bowl and flare the paper out horizontally so that it is not over the flame. Use a long taper to light the candle, and never leave burning candles unattended.

- Stand the glass in the middle of the square and pull the paper up around it, ensuring that the base is flat and pleating the paper at the rim.
- Tie your chosen cord or ribbon around the paper wrapping just above the rim of the glass so that it cannot slip down, and flare the paper out slightly.

- To avoid getting the paper wet, use a baster or a funnel to fill the small glasses with water once they are in position.
- The shortness of the flower stems makes these displays particularly long lasting; they also provide a good way of extending the life of flowers that have been left over from fading larger displays.

Alternatives with *poppies*

A more vibrant effect can be achieved by using poppies, here the brilliant scarlet Oriental poppy *Papaver orientale* 'Beauty of Livermere', whose papery petals will suit your dining table setting. You could also have a different coloured poppy or rose in each wrapped glass. The stems of all poppies must be heat treated (*see p.178*) after they are cut to length; they will then last for several days.

ROSE-PETAL COCKTAILS

TO ADD A TOUCH of glamour to a special lunch, dinner, or reception, simply stand petal-filled cocktail glasses at each place setting, next to the wine glasses. I like it if each of the "cocktails" is different, but they could just as easily all have the same flowers and colours. For a frothy topping, finish with a spray of lime-green lady's mantle (*Alchemilla mollis*).

Ingredients

Rosa 'Enigma'

Rosa 'Vicky Brown'

Rosa 'Valerie'

Rosa 'Anne Marie'

Alchemilla mollis

Black olive

FILLING THE GLASSES

- Simply twist off enough flower petals to fill the cocktail glasses and pile them in – either randomly or arranged to resemble a layered drink or an exotic flower.
- If you wish, place a silver cocktail stick with a black olive in each glass.
- These petal "cocktails" can be made a couple of hours in advance. If kept in a cool place, such as the salad crisper in a refrigerator, they will keep for longer. Once out, they will last for an evening.
- Gypsophila can be used as an alternative to alchemilla as a frothy topping.
- To continue the theme, sprinkle some rose petals on the salad – they taste as good as they look. Other edible flowers are nasturtiums, tuberous begonias, and borage. In spring try apple, cherry, and pear blossom, primroses, and other coloured polyanthus and violets.

NOCTURNE IN BROWN

SOMETIMES IT IS THE FLOWERS that inspire an arrangement and sometimes it is the container. This dark brown jug with its old rose patterning cries out for an intense arrangement. The green and black of the kangaroo paw (*Anigozanthos*), together with alder catkin and nut twigs (*Alnus glutinosa*) and little maroon-leaved "pineapples" (*Ananas nanus*), accentuate the luminous glow of the dark orange roses (*Rosa* 'Lambada') and mustard-coloured orchids (*Arachnadendron*).

Ingredients

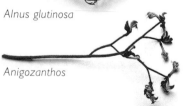

Alnus glutinosa

Anigozanthos

Arachnadendron

Rosa 'Lambada'

Ananas nanus

MAINTAIN THE DISPLAY

• Prolong the life of the roses and kangaroo paw by giving the stems a good drink in deep water before placing them in the arrangement.

• If any of the roses begin to droop, give the stems the hot water treatment (*see p.179*). This will encourage them to start taking up water again.

• Keep the jug topped up with water, and once every three days replace the water in the vase completely.

• At the end of the life of the arrangement, retain and air dry the kangaroo paw and alder twigs. Then you can combine the two to create a simple but stunning new display.

Alternative with *old variety roses*

My favourite roses are the old varieties that are highly scented, very double, and with the darkest velvety red and purple petals, such as 'Cardinal de Richelieu', 'Tuscany Superb', and 'Souvenir du Docteur Jamain'. Here I have substituted roses with almost black petals for the dark orange blooms, to create an even more striking arrangement. A little sinister in appearance, it would make an ideal Halloween display.

BASKET OF SWEET WILLIAMS

SWEET WILLIAMS have long enjoyed the reputation of being sweet-smelling, but I can only ever discern the faintest of perfumes from them. Here, a weathered terracotta basket plays host to several sweet Williams (*Dianthus barbatus* Monarch Series) in a cheerful range of pinks and white, mixed with variegated leaves of *Euonymus fortunei* 'Silver Queen' and the pink-flowering *Escallonia* 'Donard Seedling'.

ARRANGING THE FLOWERS

- As terracotta is porous, you will need to line the container with a plastic bowl or sheet plastic.
- Wedge some soaked wet foam firmly into the bottom of the container.
- Nearly fill the container with water to which is added a few drops of bleach.
- Remove from the sweet Williams all the green leaves that fall below the water level. Although it is difficult to get all the leaves off the stems, it is well worth the extra effort because they rot quickly in water.
- Arrange the sweet Williams, euonymus leaves, and escallonia stems, encouraging them to extend wide of the container.
- Top up the water level daily.

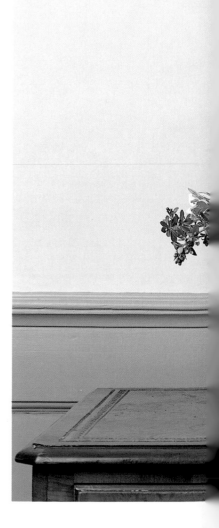

Alternative with *scarlet*

In this arrangement, I have mixed sweet Williams in scarlet and salmon with silvery green euonymus foliage and the pink escallonia. Overall, the impact is much more pronounced than that of the original pink and white display. Red and green stand opposite each other on the colour wheel (*see pp.10–11*), and this always has the effect of intensifying both colours.

Ingredients

Euonymus fortunei 'Silver Queen'

Dianthus barbatus Monarch Series

Dianthus barbatus Monarch Series

Dianthus barbatus Monarch Series

Escallonia 'Donard Seedling'

TEACUP POSIES

THE SIMPLEST IDEAS are often the best: these crackle-glazed cups and saucers make perfect containers for a mix of cottage flowers and herbs to display on a window sill. Little arrangements can be made with cuttings from the garden and look good with harmonious or clashing colours.

Here, all the cups combine chrysanthemums with other flowers: on the left with golden rod (*Solidago*) and China asters (*Callistephus*); in front with flowering mint (*Mentha*) and golden rod; and on the right with cow parsley (*Anthriscus*) and sweet-smelling, shocking-pink freesias.

Ingredients

Chrysanthemum 'Tedcha'

Mentha longifolia

Freesia 'Pink Marble'

Callistephus chinensis Princess Series

Solidago 'Goldenmosa'

Anthriscus sylvestris

Brassica

FILLING THE CUPS

• Because the cups' sides slope outwards, the flowers need to be held in. Attach a prong to the inside base of each cup with florist's adhesive clay, then press onto it a disc of 2.5cm- (1in-) thick, soaked wet foam, shaped to fit the bottom of the cup.
• Fill the cups with water and arrange the flowers in the soaked wet foam.

• Choose flowers that complement each other: the chrysanthemums and asters have daisy flowers with dark centres, golden rod and cow parsley lighten the arrangements, and freesias and mint have delicious scents.
• Ornamental cabbages (*Brassica*) provide interesting foliage, but, if these are not available, any leaves can be used.

WINTRY BASKET

IT IS ALWAYS A PLEASURE to give and receive flowers in winter and this basket, decorated with seasonal greenery and containing flowers that evoke the beauty of winter's snow and ice, would make a glorious gift. The blooms jostling in this woven vine basket are the exquisite white *Anemone coronaria* 'The Bride', framed by willow and feathery twigs of the Austrian pine (*Pinus nigra*). As a gift, this basket is simplicity itself.

BUILDING UP THE BASKET

- Weave twigs of contorted willow into the spaces between the vine stems of the basket to make it look a little wilder.
- Line the basket with a firm, waterproof container – it will not show, so do not worry about its appearance.
- Wedge a 2.5cm (1in) layer of soaked wet foam into the base of the basket to hold the flowers in place and to help prolong their life.
- Insert the flowers: let them crowd one another but without damaging the petals.
- Place the pine twigs in the container, saving a few to tie into the outer edge of the basket, along with wired pieces of reindeer moss.

Ingredients

Reindeer moss

Pinus nigra

Anemone coronaria 'The Bride'

Alternative with *holly*

I have taken out some of the anemones and replaced them with red-berried holly, making the basket more appropriate for the Christmas season. The dark, glossy leaves and red berries provide an excellent foil for the delicate anemones. Remember that the holly needs to be in water or inserted into the foam. If its ends become dry, it will brown in a short time.

PRETTY IN PINK

EARLY AZALEAS AND rhododendrons provide a welcome bridge to summer. This gift basket of pink-flowering plants makes a beautiful indoor display, after which the plants can be grown outside in a flower bed or in pots. Below the standard azalea (*Rhododendron* 'Sweetheart Supreme') are the ice-pink *Rhododendron yakushimanum* 'Isadora', lovely pink winter heath (*Erica carnea* 'Vivellii'), and ivy (*Hedera*).

ARRANGING THE BASKET
- Line your chosen basket with plastic.
- Assemble the plants in their pots, then pack enough sphagnum moss into the base of the basket to raise the rims of the pots to just below the top of the basket.
- Water all the plants thoroughly by immersing them in cool, not cold, water for about ten minutes.
- Drain the pots before placing them in the basket. Keep an eye on the azalea: the first 5cm (2in) of stem should be black after watering and the plant will need water when the stem reverts to brown.
- Position the plants to your liking, concealing the pots with more moss.
- Tie a pink ribbon around the basket when the flower arranging is complete.
- These acid-soil-loving plants can be left outside in pots of ericaceous compost, but bring them in when they flower again.

Ingredients

Rhododendron 'Sweetheart Supreme'

Rhododendron yakushimanum 'Isadora'

Hedera helix

Erica carnea 'Vivellii'

TROPICAL HEATWAVE

THIS EXOTIC display, which looks particularly stunning against the sky-blue wall, brings a touch of tropical sunshine to the coolest day. The flowers, fruit, and leaves are like vividly coloured parrots in oranges, pinks, and yellows with beak, plume, and crest shapes as well as soft, velvety textures and whorls of hard-edged, spiky leaves.

Ingredients

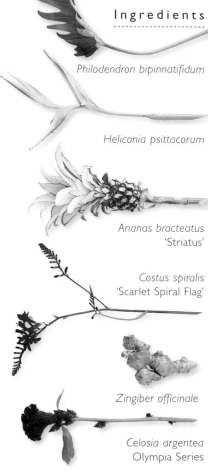

Philodendron bipinnatifidum

Heliconia psittacorum

Ananas bracteatus 'Striatus'

Costus spiralis 'Scarlet Spiral Flag'

Zingiber officinale

Celosia argentea Olympia Series

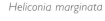

Heliconia marginata

Heliconia humilis

SUBMERGED GINGER

- Place a loose tangle of ginger roots in an elliptical glass container and three-quarters fill with water. Do not pack the ginger too tightly – the roots should support the stems without crushing them.
- Arrange the flowers and leaves in a broad fan shape so that they look as if they are growing naturally out of the ginger roots.
- Sweep upwards from left to right, creating an almost straight line with the tips of the flowers and leaves. Allow a few of the leaves to hang downwards to break the line.
- Place the largest item, the decorative pineapple, slightly left of centre to balance the arrangement.
- Change the water every three days to prevent the ginger roots from deteriorating. To avoid disturbing the arrangement, syphon off the water with a length of plastic tubing.

WATERMELON VASES

FOR A SPLASH OF BRILLIANCE at a high summer cocktail party or buffet, simply take a slice out of a watermelon and have some brilliantly coloured godetias (*Clarkia*) cascading out of its juicy flesh. With a skin that can be mottled with markings like a lizard's back, and sumptuous red flesh, the watermelon is unsurpassed where colouring is concerned. Continue the theme by serving watermelon margarita cocktails, and a non-alcoholic melon punch.

Ingredients

Clarkia amoena

Clarkia amoena

Watermelon

PREPARING THE MELON

• Find the side of the watermelon on which it will sit most steadily. Remove a slice that comprises about one-fifth of the fruit – this is for you to eat!

• Choose flowers with fairly stiff stems to push easily into the melon flesh. Godetias work well with their brilliantly coloured, papery flowers that look almost artificial.

• You can use other melons apart from watermelons – those with yellow, ribbed grey-green, or beige skins, for example, but I think that they look best with autumnal arrangements.

• Other flowers that you might consider using instead of godetia are scarlet and pink freesias, roses in mauves and creams, gypsophila, eustoma (especially the ice pink ones), gaillardias, sweet peas, small flowered orchids – the brilliant purple ones are terrific – or poppies.

CAPE GREENS

IN THE RUGGEDLY BEAUTIFUL Cape peninsula in South Africa, over 9,000 species of the vegetation known as fynbos grow, despite the difficult terrain, poor soil, and harsh weather. Bunches of these Cape greens are exported all over the world, together with proteas, heathers, and banksias. Made with a mixture of these plants, this wild-looking arrangement in a mellowed, copper creamer looks particularly good in a relaxed, rustic setting.

Ingredients

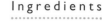

Rumex obtusifolius

Berzelia abrotanoides

Leucadendron laxum

FILLING THE BOWL

• Fynbos lasts extremely well, but with so much plant material in the arrangement it will use up a great deal of water. As a precaution, add a few drops of bleach to the water and top up the bowl regularly.
• Wedge a layer of soaked wet foam into the bowl: this is necessary as the material is arranged standing upright, and needs some support until most of it is in place.
• Keep most of the stems almost vertical, just slightly bending some of the flowers and greens outwards towards the edges to give the rim of the container a softer look. You need to get a good balance of groups of textured greenery, with some of the more imposing flowers, cones, and foliage interspersed.
• This could be arranged as an all-round display to go on a coffee table, or as a three-quarters display for a side table, where the front and sides will have more importance than the very back.

Leucadendron platyspermum

Leucadendron laxum

Erica bicolor

Alternative with *yarrow*

For some extra colour in this alternative arrangement, I have added yarrow (*Achillea*), which, together with the rust-coloured dock seed spires (*Rumex obtusifolius*), seems to have a "rough-and-tumble" affinity with the scrubby South African plants. The flat heads of the yarrow work particularly well with the intricate textures of the other plants.

Erica baccans

FRUITS AND FOLIAGE

IN THIS AUTUMNAL DISPLAY, rosehips (*Rosa moyesii*) jostle with blackberries (*Rubus fruticosus*), while guelder rose (*Viburnum opulus*) sings out against Chinese lanterns (*Physalis*) and the hot red seed pods of castor oil plant (*Ricinus communis*). The golden-green leaves of the Chinese lanterns lift the oranges and blacks of the berries and echo the green of the bowl – an excellent colour to offset berries. This display looks particularly good in a conservatory or on a garden table where it can be seen from indoors.

A NOTE OF CAUTION

- Although this display looks good enough to eat, all parts of the castor oil plant are poisonous, so keep the arrangement out of the reach of small children.
- Castor oil plant can irritate skin; take care when arranging.
- Blackberries will stain when they drop – another good reason to keep this display outside. Indoors, take care over its positioning, or stand it on a tray.

Alternative with *red foliage*

Replacing the Chinese lanterns with red autumnal beech foliage creates quite a different effect. The colours are still lifted by the green of the bowl beneath, but now the tones within the tapestry of leaves and fruits are richer and more moody. The greener display suggests a sunny autumn morning; the rusty arrangement is like a dusky autumn evening.

Ingredients

Viburnum opulus

Hydrangea 'Preziosa'

Physalis alkekengi

Ricinus communis

Rosa moyesii

Rubus fruticosus

EXOTIC CASCADE

THIS TOWER OF DANGLING exotic flowers makes an imposing floor display for a grand occasion. The tall basket allows heliconias and love-lies-bleeding (*Amaranthus caudatus*) to hang down without obstruction. The heliconias have extraordinary green and orange bracts, like a series of parrots' beaks, that last for a couple of weeks. Love-lies-bleeding, with its tassels spilling out, is a perfect partner. Papyrus heads (*Cyperus papyrus*), palm fronds (*Dypsis*), and golden-green, velvety kangaroo paw (*Anigozanthos*) complete the striking show.

BUILD THE TOWER

• Good containers to consider for an arrangement like this are galvanized florist's buckets or even elegant umbrella stands, suitably lined. The whole display comes to some 1.5m (5ft) in height when completed.

• The tall, narrow shape is inherently unstable, so it is vital that the container is weighted well at the bottom: here, a tall, cylindrical vase of just about the same diameter as the basket and two-thirds the height of it sits on top of four bricks in the bottom of the basket.

• Take care to keep the arrangement balanced as you build it: if all the heavy, dangling heliconias were to one side, the basket would fall, even with the bricks.

• Start with the longest heliconia dangling lowest in the display and gradually build the display upwards.

• These tall palm fronds had to have nearly 60cm (2ft) of their leaflets removed to give them long "stalks" for arranging.

• The love-lies-bleeding leaves will die first. Remove them, and the rest of the display will last for another ten days.

Ingredients

Amaranthus caudatus

Heliconia nutans

Anigozanthos flavidus

Cyperus papyrus

Dypsis lutescens

SHADES OF PALE

A GENTLE DOME of white and blush flowers stands serenely beside a glass plate of papery garlic bulbs and ribbed mushrooms. Perfumed mock orange (*Philadelphus* 'Belle Etoile') and *Phlox paniculata* 'Fujiyama' jostle with *Eustoma grandiflorum* and *Scabiosa caucasica* 'Miss Willmott', while white spires of *Lysimachia clethroides* erupt in every direction.

ARRANGING THE FLOWERS

• Place a small disc of soaked wet foam on a florist's spike in the bottom of a pure white glass bowl, or alternatively in a china one. The foam will help to hold the stems in place as you arrange them.
• Place the stems of mock orange, then the phlox and scabious, turning the bowl to see how they look from all round.
• Add the large, ice-pink eustoma flowers, aiming for an informal but balanced look; then add the lysimachia spires, allowing them to cascade out of the arrangement.
• Cut off dying mock orange and eustoma flowers to encourage new buds to appear.

Ingredients

Lysimachia clethroides

Phlox paniculata 'Fujiyama'

Eustoma grandiflorum Heidi Series

Philadelphus 'Belle Etoile'

Scabiosa caucasica 'Miss Willmott'

Allium sativum

ARRANGING THE GARLIC

- Find a plate that complements the vase you have chosen – the one I used here features swirls of clear and white glass.
- Lay out the garlic bulbs: the blush visible through their papery skin echoes the tinge of the mock orange flowers.
- Add the ribbed oyster mushrooms. If kept out for only a few hours, they may be refrigerated and eaten the following day.

BREATH OF SPRING

LILY-OF-THE-VALLEY (*Convallaria majalis*) has one of the most evocative of all scents: for me it conjures up my childhood breath of pleasure as, each late spring, their tiny flowers exploded with fragrance beneath opening azaleas. This graceful curve of test tubes, each holding a few delicate stems, refreshes the flowers and leaves so that their short-lived beauty and piercingly delicious perfume can be enjoyed by all.

CREATING THE CONTAINER

* For this display, you'll need 15 test tubes and a coil of plastic-coated garden wire.
* Cut two lengths of garden wire, each 1.5m (5ft) long. (If you want to wire together more or fewer test tubes, adjust the wire lengths accordingly.)
* Find the middle point of one wire by folding it in half, and bend it around one test tube, about 1cm (½in) below the rim.
* Twist the ends of the wire until the tube is held firmly in place by the wire loop.

* Twist the wire ends a further six or seven times to create a 2cm (¾in) gap between the first tube and the next one.
* Take in the second test tube by twisting the wire ends around it, make another width of twisted wire, and continue until all the tubes are connected. Leave about 1.25cm (½in) of wire at the end, bent down the side of the final tube.
* Repeat with the second wire, starting 2.5cm (1in) up from the bottom of the test tubes and keeping the tubes parallel.

Alternative with *columbines*

Having wired up your row of test tubes, you can bend it into any shape, such as a triangle, square, or the circle shown here. Columbines (*Aquilegia*) are incredibly beautiful, underrated flowers that are available in late spring or early summer in an extraordinary range of mostly pastel colours. Another choice is strawberry-perfumed mock orange (*Philadelphus coronarius*). Arrange two or three stems of either type in each test tube.

Ingredients

Convallaria majalis

WATSONIA SPRAY

ORANGE AND LIME-GREEN are a particularly luscious combination; lying close to each other on the colour wheel (*see pp.10–11*), they are both harmonious and uplifting. Here, orange watsonias (*Watsonia pillansii*) appear almost luminous against a chartreuse chrysanthemum cultivar (*Chrysanthemum* 'Green Spider'). Great swathes of watsonia grow in the fynbos habitats of southern Africa – a wonderful source of many extraordinary blooms. The flowers form an elegant fountain, rising from a froth of spider chrysanthemums in a tall, bronze-based glass vase, and are perfect for a side table.

COMBINING FLOWERS

• Watsonias, which originate from South Africa, are sometimes hard to find. However, both montbretia (*Crocosmia*) and gladioli belong to the same family and many forms of these could be substituted, if necessary, to achieve the same effect.

• The larger flowered chrysanthemums can be difficult to use as they sometimes appear heavy and clumsy. One solution is to treat the flower heads almost like foliage, as here, keeping them close to the vase, with more delicate flowers springing from them. This is both easy and effective

• Take care not to damage the base and largest petals of the chrysanthemums whe arranging them; once a chrysanthemum starts to disintegrate, all the other petals quickly follow suit.

Alternative with *purple*

To achieve a more muted effect, combine the watsonias with deeper, richer colours, such as the plum of the chrysanthemum 'Sentry' used here. This or the main arrangement could also look good with an orange gladiolus such as 'Little Darling', which is bright orange with a yellow throat, or the frilly, brilliant orange 'Firestorm'. There are also magnificent *Crocosmia* cultivars, such as 'Firebird' and 'Lucifer', both bright red, that make a strong impact.

Ingredients

Watsonia pillansii

Chrysanthemum 'Green Spider'

MAGNOLIA WREATH

FREQUENTLY THE SIMPLEST of things work out to be the best. This wreath, shaped like the ancient Greek and Roman headdresses, consists of nothing but the leaves and fruit of bull bay (*Magnolia grandiflora*). The evergreen leaves of what I think is one of the most beautiful of all trees have glossy, rich green tops and brown felty backs, making a very special contrast. The fruits look like fleshy pine cones and drop rich red seeds as they ripen – in winter the trees have both leaves and fruit. This wreath lasts very well and can be hung either traditionally on the front door, or on an inside door to welcome people into a room.

MAKING THE WREATH

- Cut a strip of chicken wire about 112cm (3½ft) long and 10cm (4in) wide, stuff it with dry sphagnum moss (or wet moss if the wreath will hang outside), and form it into a tube about 5cm (2in) in diameter.
- Bend the tube into the wreath shape, or a circle if you prefer, and use mossing wire to join the ends at the apex; attach a stub wire hanging loop at this point.
- Cut some 10cm (4in) medium-gauge stub wires and fold them into a U shape.

- Use these to wire together groups of three leaves each in a fan shape, placing some green side up and some brown.
- Lay the moss-filled tube on a flat surface with the top end away from you. Starting at the top, arrange the trios of leaves by layering them down the sides of the wreath with their tips pointing towards the top. Secure the leaves by pushing the ends of the stub wires through the moss then bending them back. Finish off the base of the wreath with a "rosette" of overlapping leaves, radiating out from a central point.
- Wire in some fruits, keeping the best for the centre of the "rosette". Conceal any exposed wire tube with wired single leaves.

Ingredients

Magnolia grandiflora

FLORAL ICE BOWL

ONE OF THE MOST striking ways of presenting flowers is to capture them in ice. The simplest method is to freeze a single flower in an ice cube, but the more adventurous can make an iced flower bowl or a champagne bucket to keep in the freezer, ready for a special occasion. The effect of vibrantly coloured flowers, trapped in a glass-like bowl, is enchanting, while the transience of the display adds to its allure. Here, I have used feathery coriander leaves and the flowers of a vivid blue iris (*Iris* 'Professor Blaauw').

Ingredients

Iris 'Professor Blaauw'

Coriandrum sativum

MAKING THE BOWL

• Take two glass bowls: one just over 2.5cm (1in) smaller in diameter than the other. Half-fill the larger bowl with water.

• Place the smaller bowl in the larger one and fill it with water until its base is floating approximately 2cm (¾in) above the bottom of the larger bowl.

• Dry the sides of the outer bowl and the rim of the inner. Hold the inner bowl in place by placing two pieces of tape at right angles over the two bowls.

• Carefully insert flowers and foliage between the bowls, using a skewer to gently push them into position. Leave the bowls overnight in the freezer.

• To unmould the ice bowl, float the two glass bowls in cold water and add cold water to the small inner bowl. After a minute or two, gently lift out the inner bowl. Invert and remove the larger bowl.

Alternative with *champagne bottle*

You can make a champagne ice bucket in exactly the same way as the ice bowl, using two small bucket-shaped vessels as moulds, one slightly larger than the other. Avoid using any poisonous flowers or leaves, in case someone decides to break off a piece of ice and eat it.

ARUM LILY FAN

WHEN USING GLASS containers, consider not only the shape that the flowers and foliage make above the water but also how the stalks look under water. In this arrangement of apricot arum lilies (*Zantedeschia*), gold-splashed elaeagnus, and golden holly berries (*Ilex verticillata*), the stems come together at the bottom in a fan shape. The result is a dramatic display, perfect for a narrow side table or a window sill.

ARRANGE THE STEMS
• Take particular care when handling elaeagnus as its spines are sharp.
• If possible, fill the hollow stems of the arum lilies with water (*see p.178*) to prolong their display.
• Start by arranging the arum lily stems on the right-hand side, propping them up against the side of the vase.
• Next place more arum lilies on the left, with a long stem extending to the base of the vase on the right.
• Now place the berried stems in a curve below the arum lilies, with the elaeagnus in a curve below these.

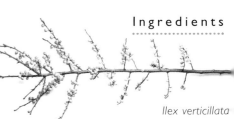

Ingredients

Ilex verticillata

Alternative with *roses*

In the main arrangement, the colour of the berries echoes that of the arum lilies, creating a harmonious effect. Here, some small, bright red roses have been added to give more vibrancy. They have all been kept to much the same length, shorter than the arum lilies and berries but longer than the elaeagnus, to create distinct bands of colour across the width of the fan.

Zantedeschia 'Dusty Pink

Elaeagnus pungens 'Maculata

VASE OF ANTHURIUMS

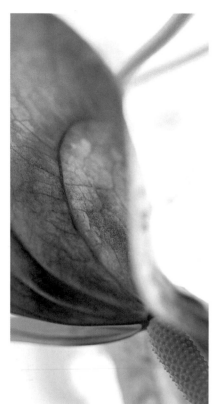

THE PART THAT A VASE PLAYS in a display can never be underestimated, and this vase is a winner in several important ways. It is striking in itself: the blue is reminiscent of tropical seas, while the fine red stripe adds interest and gives it an airy elegance. The narrow neck helps the flowers to almost arrange themselves and means that a few flowers will fill the vase, making it useful for everyday displays as well as special occasions. In this display, green-and-crimson anthuriums float above pale-veined green-and-cream decorative cabbage (*Brassica*) leaves: an exotic plant and a garden vegetable might seem an unlikely mix, but the result is stunning.

PREPARING THE MATERIAL

- Anthuriums need to be conditioned by standing in deep water for several hours before arranging (*see pp.176–177*).
- Cabbage stems can quickly begin to rot and smell unpleasant. To prolong their life, put a few drops of bleach in the water before you create the arrangement.
- After two or three days, empty out the water in the vase and replace with fresh: it is quite easy to grip all the flowers in the vase together while you do this.

- As the anthuriums last for a fairly long time, remove the cabbage when it is past its sell-by date, and replace with other foliage – maybe some tropical philodendron leaves, or a spiky grass leaf.
- The shape of this vase makes arranging easy, the narrow neck holding the stems in position without the need for foam or additional support. Do check, however, that a vase is heavy enough to balance a top-heavy arrangement.

Alternative with *nerines*

Here the same anthuriums have had their stems cut so that they huddle close to the rim of the vase. They are interspersed with nerines, whose intense scarlet petals possess a beautiful crystalline quality. Set off by the translucent blue of the vase and picking up its red veining, the combination is electrifying. Another variation might be to use hosta or bergenia leaves instead of the cabbage.

Ingredients

Anthurium andraeanum 'Trinidad'

Brassica Northern Lights Series

RADIANT SPIRES

AFRICAN CONTAINERS, one of hide and one of wood, set off tall, glowing spires of *Bulbinella hookeri*, a native of South Africa and New Zealand. In the hide pot (*left*), the feathery foliage and yellow heads of banksia (*Grevillea robusta*) mix with the orange spires; in a wooden pot, brilliant pot marigolds (*Calendula officinalis*) meld with the yellow spires.

Alternative with *asters*

While yellow and orange blooms harmonize easily, the addition of rich purple Michaelmas daisies (*Aster novi-belgii* 'Chequers') creates a violent contrast, making the marigolds appear even brighter and sunnier. This is because the two colours are opposite each other in the colour wheel (*see pp. 10–11*). Late summer is a good time for this display because bulbinellas, marigolds, and Michaelmas daisies are all in season then.

Ingredients

Grevillea robusta

Bulbinella hookeri

Bulbinella hookeri

Calendula officinalis

ARRANGING THE FLOWERS

• Check that rustic containers are watertight: in the case of the hide vase, I placed a cylindrical glass vase inside rather than using a plastic lining that could be pierced by the banksia.

• To improve the appearance of the marigolds and make them last longer, remove most of the leafy side-shoots and some of the larger leaves.

• Place the orange bulbinella spires and banksia at roughly the same height.

• Allow the yellow bulbinella spires to dominate the crown of the arrangement, with marigolds forming the lower tiers.

FAIRY-LIGHT TREE

ARRANGEMENTS THAT BRING a smile seem especially appropriate for the festive season, and this concoction of lights and winter greenery provides a humorous slant on the traditional Christmas tree. This "tree" has a trunk made from a hurricane lamp filled with fir (*Abies*) and the ribbon-like leaves of sedge (*Carex*), topped by fairy lights. The effect is stunning, but simple to create; it is also absolutely safe as no water is involved. Displays with lights look wonderful in windows or on a hall table.

MAKING THE TREE

• Tape the wire of a set of 50 fairy lights down the back of a pot that is about 12cm (5in) wider in diameter than the hurricane lamp glass. Pack dry foam into the pot.
• Pass the fairy lights through the glass from the bottom to the top. Embed the glass in the dry foam in the pot.
• Fill the glass with long-lasting fir, sedge, and dried hibiscus lanterns.
• Pile the lights on top of the glass to form the crown of the "tree". If necessary, support them on twigs anchored in the top of the hurricane lamp.
• Surround the tree with dried carpet moss (*Mnium hornum*) and a few hibiscus lanterns.

Ingredients

Mnium hornum

Abies procera

Hibiscus sabdariffa

Cryptomeria japonica 'Cristata'

Carex oshimensis 'Evergold'

SPRING BLOSSOM

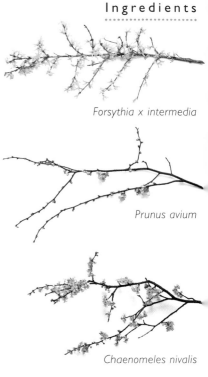

Forsythia x intermedia

Prunus avium

Chaenomeles nivalis

JUXTAPOSING THE DELICACY of spring blossom with a heavy lead vase may seem odd, but in fact the flowers seem to float up out of the silvery grey container. This combination of delicate wild gean (*Prunus avium*), white ornamental quince (*Chaenomeles*), and clear yellow forsythia looks ethereal against a pale wall or against the sky on an upstairs window sill.

Alternative with *viburnum*

This more eye-catching effect is achieved by adding flowers of the snowball bush, *Viburnum macrocephalum*. Its pompoms of spring-green fading to white make the display look very fresh. Remove all the leaves from the snowball bush stems, as they would detract from the airiness of the bare twigs. For a softer alternative, replace the bright yellow forsythia with the pale lemon of *Forsythia suspensa* or *Forsythia* 'Spring Glory'.

FORM A TWIG OUTLINE

• Use the shapes of the branches to form the structure of the arrangement: forsythia tends to grow quite straight, but the stems of the other ingredients offer more interesting and intricate lines.

• Avoid using too many branches: the arrangement should have an airy feel and not appear too crowded.

• Stand back frequently to check the overall shape and keep rearranging the branches until the balance is just right: if too many of the twigs cross, the tracery will look busy rather than lacy.

• All of this material has a good vase life, particularly the forsythia; the delicate gean blossom will be the first to fade, but even this lasts reasonably well.

BLUE LAGOON

THE CONTAINER USED for this vivid display is a beechwood laundry box with a wok wedged inside it to hold the water. An edging of hosta leaves provides a margin around the "pool", which is packed with bright blue irises. A solitary, dark red rose (*Rosa* The Dark Lady ('Ausbloom')) emerges from amidst the irises, to great dramatic effect.

Ingredients

Hosta 'Frosted Jade'

Iris 'Professor Blaauw'

Rosa The Dark Lady ('Ausbloom')

PREPARING THE POOL

- Make sure that the inner container is securely wedged in place. Attach a block of soaked wet foam to some prongs at its base to hold the arrangement in place.
- Cover the outer rim of the container with hosta leaves, and cram the inside with irises, pushing their stems into the wet foam at the base.
- Add a single flower in a contrasting colour to the arrangement.

Alternative with *alchemilla*

The idea for this arrangement came to me as I considered the vivid green duckweed that appears on the surface of my water-filled troughs. Here a froth of alchemilla flowers covers the surface, while a lone 'New Dawn' rose floats serenely on the surface like a water lily. This arrangement should be set at ground level, as it has to be looked down on for the best effect.

ORCHIDS IN BARK

THERE IS SOMETHING extraordinary about orchids, with their intriguing waxy flowers, strange shapes, and often sinister look, yet they are captivatingly beautiful. In this bark-covered basket I have used two kinds, a moth orchid (*Phalaenopsis hybrid*) and a slipper orchid (*Paphiopedilum hybrid*). The winter foliage I have used on the basket is far removed from the orchids' natural environment, but it seems to work, making a link with the conifer bark on the basket.

CREATING THE DISPLAY

• Find a wicker basket to hold the orchids and line it with plastic.

• Cover the basket with bark. Laceback pine (*Pinus bungeana*) is good, but any bark will serve. Cut the bark about 9cm (3½in) wide and a little higher than the basket, leaving rough edges on top.

• Tie two lengths of mossing wire to the basket, about one-third and two-thirds of the way down, avoiding the lining, and leaving some spare wire at the tied end.

• Fit the pieces of bark around the basket

so that they slightly overlap. When you are happy with the look, bind the upper wire tightly around them and tie off against the end that you left uncut. Repeat with the

lower wire, then trim off the long ends.

• Fill the basket with sphagnum moss and slot in the orchids in their pots (three plants of each type). Tuck some noble fir (*Abies procera*) or other fir in and around the pots. Wire in a few small fir cones.

• Conceal the wires holding the bark with raffia or rustic-looking ribbon.

• To water the orchids, remove the pots from the basket and plunge them in rainwater up to the rim. Leave until completely saturated then allow to drain before returning them to the bark basket.

Ingredients

Pine cone

Pinus bungeana bark

Abies procera

Paphiopedilum hybrid

Phalaenopsis hybrid

LATE-SUMMER HARMONY

A FROTH OF PALE, delicate colours shimmers above an opaque white glass vase with cerulean blue decorations. Icy pink nerines, clear blue delphiniums, white phlox, yellow marigolds (*Tagetes*), and pale green foliage – how harmoniously these spring-like colours mix, even with late-summer flowers. The trumpet shape of the vase makes arranging the flowers easy – it is simply a matter of balancing colours, shapes, and textures in an informal look. A few tall delphiniums stand up out of the arrangement, while the nerines cluster below the centre.

MIXING THE COLOURS

• Remember to use appropriate amounts of the different colours: softer shades of blue will retreat while the stronger pink and yellow will stand out.
• An arrangement composed entirely of pastel colours will have a very soft look: here, the addition of just a small amount of bright orange silkweed (*Asclepias*) significantly sharpens the look.
• Spread the various colours so that they are well balanced but do not make patterns. It is all too easy to produce a straight line of one colour within an arrangement; break it by simply moving just one flower.
• Remove any leaves that would be under water: those that are overlooked will quickly decay and start to affect all the other flowers (*see p.177*).
• When using a tall, narrow vase, make sure that it is heavy enough to balance the weight of the arrangement.

Ingredients

Delphinium 'Cressida'

Tagetes Antigua Series

Nerine bowdenii 'Alba'

Phlox 'Kelly's Eye'

Phlox paniculata 'Fujiyama'

Curcuma aeruginosa

Lysimachia vulgaris

Asclepias tuberosa

MINIATURE GARDEN

THIS MAGICAL DISPLAY in a glass aquarium is reminiscent of the nineteenth-century passion for growing plants in glass containers. Here, however, I have used cut flowers and leaves. A mossy bank is studded with winter and early spring flowers such as Christmas roses (*Helleborus niger*), sweet-scented grape hyacinths (*Muscari*), lily-of-the-valley (*Convallaria majalis*), and parrot tulips (*Tulipa cultivars*). In an autumn garden I might use pieces of gnarled wood, sprigs of berried twigs, and spiky beech capsules (*Fagus*). The arrangement could go on a side table or even in the centre of a large dining table.

FILL THE TANK

- The aquarium is 40 x 22cm (16 x 9in). In a smaller tank, use smaller flowers.
- Cover the bottom with a 4cm (1½in) layer of soaked wet foam, leaving a 1cm (½in) gap around the edges. Fill the gap with strips of carpet moss, with more carpet moss over the foam. If the tank is to be seen only from one side, mound the foam and moss up towards the back.
- Place the flowers, making holes with a skewer for those with fragile stalks. Use tree heather (*Erica arborea*) and wired bunches of acorus for miniature bushes.
- Water the garden frequently – it is a surprisingly thirsty display. The hellebores last least well, but could easily be replaced by chrysanthemums or grape hyacinths.

Ornamental cabbage (*Brassica*)

Muscari armeniacum

Convallaria majalis

Chrysanthemum spray cultivar

Acorus calamus 'Variegatus'

Erica arborea

Helleborus niger

Tulipa 'Webber's Parrot'

TEATIME DISPLAYS

IT IS ALWAYS INTERESTING to adapt everyday household objects as containers for flowers. Here, a sleek modern kettle and old-fashioned china teapot act as perfect alternative vases on a side table. The highly polished kettle reflects the brightly coloured poppies (*Papaver nudicaule* cultivars) that cascade around the rim: the opening is quite narrow, but the eccentric shapes of poppies can be chosen to fall in an attractive way.

HEAT TREATING POPPIES

- All types of poppies need to be heat treated (*see p.178*); re-treat the ends of bought poppies if cut.
- The simplest way to heat treat flowers intended for a kettle is to stand them in 2.5cm (1in) of almost boiling water in the kettle for about four minutes, then simply top up with cold water.
- If the poppies that you buy at a flower shop have been heat treated, this will probably be indicated on their wrapping. Such flowers should not be cut before arranging. If your arrangement requires that the stems be cut, then you will have to heat treat the flowers again yourself after cutting them to the required length.
- Once they have been conditioned and arranged, poppies last surprisingly well – up to seven days. Their fragile looks belie a stout constitution.

Alternative with *teapot*

The same basic idea can be used to create displays of a quite different character. This nineteenth-century Staffordshire teapot is a more gentle affair than the ultra-modern kettle, and is home here to some beautifully scented sweet peas (*Lathyrus odoratus* 'Wiltshire Ripple'). Unlike the poppies, which hug the kettle, these sweet peas are arranged in an airy mound that floats up out of the teapot.

Ingredients

Papaver nudicaule 'Summer Breeze'

GLITTERING SWAG

Pinus sylvestris cones

Pinus strobus cone

Larix decidua

Papaver somniferum (dried)

LICHEN-COVERED twigs of European larch (*Larix decidua*) are just right for swagging a window, doorway, or a fireplace that will not be used for fires over the Christmas holiday. I have sprinkled the twigs with tiny silver star spangles to make them glitter, and decorated them with glittering dried heads of the opium poppy (*Papaver somniferum*), plus a mixture of pine cones and some large turquoise and blue glass spheres.

FESTIVE FIREPLACE

• To attach the swag to a stone or marble fireplace, fit a long wire loop tightly around the length of the mantelshelf (*right*). You can then tie the swag to the wire. For wooden fireplaces, use the same method, or attach with small tacks.

• Make the two side drops by binding larch branches together with dark-coloured mossing wire. They should be long enough to reach two-thirds of the way down the sides of the fireplace.

• Spray-paint the poppy heads and pine cones in blue and silver to complement the colour of the glass spheres.

• Randomly wire some of the poppy heads and pine cones onto the larch side drops.

• Take the completed side drops outside

and spray them with photo mount, then immediately sprinkle them with the tiny glittering silver stars. They are now ready to hang from the fireplace wire.

• Repeating the technique used for the side drops, make two larger twig sections for the top of the fireplace, each just over half the length of the mantelshelf. Select the branches by holding them in position and appraising their shapes before making up the sections.

• Secure the twig sections to the wire, placing them top to top, so that they fan upwards and intertwine attractively at the centre of the mantelpiece.

• Add the glass spheres, using their hooks to wire them into the twigs and placing them so that each side looks different.

FLOATING FLOWERS

WATER IS AN essential feature in any garden: in my London garden, I have a small pool, two water tanks, two old stone drinking troughs, and a couple of oil jars that I keep filled with water throughout the year. Every few days I pick some flower heads, such as these rose-pink peonies (*Paeonia* 'Globe of Light'), and float them on the water's surface, to enchanting effect.

HOW TO MAINTAIN

- Float a couple of open-cup peonies on the surface of the water in a stone trough.
- Keep duckweed in check, otherwise it will eventually take over the entire surface of water in troughs and pools. For the best effect, try to allow at least a little clear dark water to show through at the surface.
- To maintain an attractive mossy exterior on terracotta or stone plant containers, spray them with water every day.
- Lean old oil jars at an angle, fill with water, and decorate with floating flowers such as yellow tuberous begonias, pale pink roses, or some pelargonium foliage.
- Remove floating flower heads as they die and replace with fresh blooms. If you don't have enough in your garden, you could always buy a few.

Alternative with *mortar*

This marble mortar has been seconded to the garden from the kitchen. It is small and elegant – measuring only 25cm (10in) in diameter – which makes it a perfect container for a few floating flowers. Here there are two 'Purple Tiger' roses, some deep red pelargoniums, and bright blue felicia flowers. Always keep the water fresh as flower petals can very quickly produce rotting bacteria.

Ingredients

Paeonia 'Globe of Light'

OPULENT TAZZA

THIS LAVISH LOW ARRANGEMENT in a tazza (a glass wine bowl) makes an ideal centrepiece for the dinner table as it does not obscure the diners' views. To an exotic mélange of orange *Ranunculus asiaticus*, pink Eustoma grandiflorum, fragrant *Polianthes tuberosa*, deep orange *Euphorbia fulgens*, lotus seed heads (*Nelumbo nucifera*), and fig leaves (*Ficus carica*) is added black grapes, tumbling voluptuously from the glass bowl.

CREATE THE FRAMEWORK

• Fix a florist's prong to the base of the tazza with adhesive clay. Attach a piece of soaked wet foam 5cm (2in) square and 7.5cm (3in) high. Fill the tazza with water.

• Tie a bunch of grapes to each end of a length of wire and lay over the tazza. Add two more pairs of wired bunches.

• Weave in an inner circle of wire, about 5cm (2in) in from the rim. The foam and the spider's web of wires will help to hold the flowers in place as you arrange them.

Ingredients

Ficus carica

Euphorbia fulgens

Eustoma grandiflorum Heidi Series

Nelumbo nucifera

Polianthes tuberosa 'The Pearl'

Ranunculus asiaticus Turban Group

Vitis vinifera

CHEQUERED HEADS

A WONDROUS SIGHT, the snake's head fritillary (*Fritillaria meleagris*) has bell-shaped flowers patterned in chequers, ranging in colour around plum and maroon with incursions into pink, cream, and white. They look superb in this vase, which relates to their petals, along with another holding a few Christmas roses (*Helleborus niger*).

Ingredients

Fritillaria meleagris

Helleborus niger

Alternative with *tulips*

To the simple arrangement of snake's head fritillaries I have added some amazing tulips – a variety named 'Gavota' – turning out their petals to maximize their impact. Their flowers of plum, cream, and green are in the same colour range as the fritillaries, and they seem to have strayed from a seventeenth-century painting. It is always exciting to chance upon such a fascinating colour link between two flowers.

ARRANGING THE FLOWERS

• Find two containers that will happily complement each other in shape, colour, and texture, looking also for colours that harmonize with the flowers.

• Cut the stems of the fritillaries. They appear to be extremely fragile, but actuall last reasonably well once cut.

• Arrange the fritillaries quite densely wit their leaves still on the stem, encouraging the robust leaves to spring up wildly.

• Take the hellebores (Christmas roses) and stick a pin through their stems severa times just below the flower, then place them in warm water. The flowers will tak in more water and therefore last longer.

• Arrange the heads of the hellebores so that they just skim the top of their vase.

MEDITERRANEAN JAR

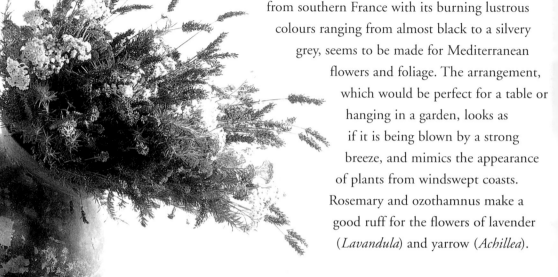

THIS TERRACOTTA jar, which is reminiscent of vessels from southern France with its burning lustrous colours ranging from almost black to a silvery grey, seems to be made for Mediterranean flowers and foliage. The arrangement, which would be perfect for a table or hanging in a garden, looks as if it is being blown by a strong breeze, and mimics the appearance of plants from windswept coasts. Rosemary and ozothamnus make a good ruff for the flowers of lavender (*Lavandula*) and yarrow (*Achillea*).

ADAPTING THE JAR

- If you see a vase or pot that you like, it is always worth buying it even if it does not immediately seem ideal for flowers. This jar, for example, has a curved base and came in a hanging sling, but it is easy to keep it upright by supporting the base on a ring of plaited raffia.

- Line porous jars with a plastic container or a sheet of plastic; take care not to pierce the latter with woody stems.
- Wedge some soaked wet foam in the jar to hold the first few stems in place.
- To make this arrangement last as long as possible, remove all the leaves from the lower parts of the stems. Adding a few drops of bleach to the water when you top it up will also help prolong its life.

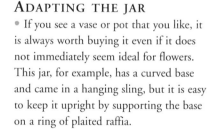

Ingredients

Rosmarinus officinalis

Ozothamnus rosmarinifolius

Achillea 'Hartington White'

Lavandula angustifolia

VIOLETS AND BLUE

LYING IN THE SPECTRUM between clear blue and the warmer hues of plum and purple, violet is a powerful colour that glows darkly but vividly – and all the more so when set off by a vibrant blue. Here, richly perfumed sweet violets (*Viola odorata*) are stunningly displayed in a tall, narrow, indigo and turquoise vase and a moon-shaped, translucent blue container, while a turquoise bowl offsets the luscious petals and intense black eyes of *Anemone coronaria* 'Mona Lisa Purple'.

Ingredients

Anemone coronaria 'Mona Lisa Purple'

Primula Polyanthus Group Crescendo Series

Viola odorata

Alternative with *primulas*

The sweet violets are retained in their intensely blue, translucent container. Next to them a turquoise bowl holds heads of deep violet polyanthus (*Primula* Polyanthus Group Crescendo Series), each flower with a bright gold centre. The polyanthus will add their own fragrance to the delightful, old-fashioned perfume of the sweet violets.

DISPLAYING THE FLOWERS

• Seek out containers in colours that will resonate with the hues of the flowers you are arranging. The original function of the containers need not deter you – for example, the asymmetrical, bright blue container housing the violets is nothing more grand than a plastic wastepaper bin.

• Arrange the anemones in their container, ensuring that they have adequate water.

• Set aside any long-stemmed leaves that have been supplied with the violets.

• Attach the short stems of the violets to wire supports, cutting the wires long enough to hold up the violets' heads just above the top of their container, with the stems trailing down inside.

• Wire short-stemmed polyanthus leaves in the same way, with their ends about 4cm (1½in) below the top of the container.

• Water the vases of violets to the brim, and top them up frequently.

ARTICHOKE BASKET

THIS BASKET of woven palm leaves is reminiscent of the globe artichoke (*Cynara scolymus*), its knobbly texture conjuring up the tight layers of bracts that surround the "choke" or flower head. In the basket, I have combined seed heads of opium poppies (*Papaver somniferum*), flower heads of sea holly (*Eryngium*), and artichokes in various stages of maturity to create a striking, low arrangement that is suitable as a table centrepiece.

MAKE A BASKET

- As the poppy leaves are short-lived, they can be replaced as they droop, or omitted.
- Artichoke heads are heavy, so it is best to use them in low displays, such as this one, for maximum stability.
- If left in the basket after the water has gone, all of the ingredients apart from the poppy leaves should dry successfully.
- *Papaver somniferum* 'Hen and Chickens' seed heads are great fun, and could be substituted for the opium poppy.

Ingredients

Cynara scolymus

Eryngium alpinum

Papaver somniferum

Alternative with *nightlight*

Take an almost open artichoke: remove the stem and hollow out from below, leaving enough flesh to hold the leaves in place. Pull out any leaves from the centre that would overlap the candle flame, and slide in a nightlight in a holder such as a shot glass.

ORCHIDS AND REEDS

FLOWERS SEEM TO ARRANGE themselves in vases of this shape but, since even the smaller-flowered cymbidium orchids can be top-heavy, these are staked with reed palm, which also adds vertical interest to the arrangement. The beautiful, warm, golden-silver patina of the vase shows off any colour, but especially green and gold as here.

ARRANGING THE ORCHIDS

• Each stem of orchid is tied to a reed stake with two short lengths of raffia; no attempt has been made to hide the raffia, which adds a textural interest of its own.

• Remove the lower orchid flowers as they start to fade: this will encourage more buds to come out further up the stem.

• Many orchids last well when cut, yet it is still important to condition them (*see pp.176-178*). Even if you buy the orchids with their stems in tubes of water, recut the ends and recondition them.

Alternative with *red*

Here, a brilliant red anemone is set against the green, intensifying both colours, which lie opposite each other on the colour wheel (*see pp.30–31*). Anemones have a superb colour range, from pure white, through pinks, to deep purples and bright reds. The black centres and halo of white at the base of each petal intensify the red even more. They will not last as long as the orchids, but can be either removed or replaced.

Ingredients

Cymbidium Kings Loch

Chamaedorea seifrizii

ROSE BOWL

A RICH GOLDEN BROWN marble bowl makes an elegant container for this display of just one type of flower – a melange of roses (*Rosa* cultivars) in peach, yellow, and pink, with just enough colour clash to add interest. The boiled-sweet hues of the roses are mouthwatering, and their scent is intoxicating too. This sumptuous display would be perfect for a church christening, placed on the floor close to the font.

FILL THE BOWL

• It is often best to arrange heavy containers like this in situ.
• Attach several prongs to the base of the bowl with adhesive clay and push on a 4cm (1½in) layer of soaked wet foam.
• Fill the bowl with sufficient water to cover the top of the foam layer.

• To prolong their lives, cut each rose stem at an angle and scrape each end (*see pp.178*). Treated in this way, the flowers should last for a week.
• Arrange the prepared rose stems in the bowl, taking care to achieve an even but seemingly random mix of colours.

• Flowers for special occasions need to be perfect for only a few hours; buy or cut roses on the point of opening a few days ahead so that they peak for the event.
• In summer, this arrangement would look stunning with full-blown peonies (*Paeonia*); in autumn, try a mix of hydrangeas.

Ingredients

Rosa 'Vivaldi'   *Rosa 'Bo'*   *Rosa 'Candy Bianca'*   *Rosa 'Gold Strike'*   *Rosa 'Pistache'*

JELLY MOULDS

THE FLUTED SHAPES of these ceramic moulds – once used for jellies and blancmanges – make them wonderful to use as vases; their creamy glaze is ideally suited to spring arrangements of scarlet-streaked, pale tulips (*Tulipa* 'Carnaval de Rio'), creamy hyacinths (*Hyacinthus orientalis*), and the fragile flowers of *Leucojum vernum*, the spring snowflake.

Ingredients

Hyacinthus orientalis 'City of Haarlem'

Tulipa 'Carnaval de Rio'

Leucojum vernum

FILL THE MOULDS

- Arranging flowers in wide-necked containers and bowls can be tricky; attach a few prongs to the base of each jelly mould with adhesive clay to help hold the first stems as they are placed.
- As tulips continue growing for several days and may lengthen considerably in the vase, cut them slightly shorter to begin with than the required eventual length.

- Tulips form very attractive shapes as they grow, but if they become too unruly, wrap them in a roll of newspaper and stand them in deep water overnight to straighten them (*see p.179*).
- Hyacinth stems bleed a glutinous sap that can encourage bacteria to grow, so be sure to add two or three drops of household bleach to the water.

HARVEST THANKSGIVING

FRUIT AND VEGETABLES are piled into a basket that has been decorated with bunches of dried flowers to make a side table display for a Thanksgiving dinner. Dried blooms, such as pink peonies (*Paeonia*), roses (*Rosa*), and lavender (*Lavandula*), combine with autumnal hops (*Humulus*), wheat (*Triticum*), and artichokes (*Cynara*). These are attached to the outside of the basket in bunches, pointing both upwards and downwards, and will all last for at least a couple of months or until they become dusty.

COVERING THE BASKET

• Choose a basket that has reasonably open wickerwork, so that the wires holding the bunches can be pushed through to the inside and secured by twisting the ends together.
• Wire all the bunches of flowers, foliage, and vegetables (*see p.184*) before beginning to cover the basket.
• Starting at one corner, attach the bunches of flowers, foliage, and vegetables, and some single wired artichokes to the basket.

Overlap the flowers as you work, but leave some parts of the basket uncovered.
• Make sure that the ends of the wires inside the basket are turned back on themselves, to avoid puncturing any fruit and vegetables that are put into the basket.
• Once you have decorated the sides, the basket is ready for a wonderful pile of fruit and vegetables. Alternatively, why not line the inside with dried moss, so the basket also looks good when empty?

Ingredients

Cynara scolymus   *Lavandula angustifolia*   *Rosa 'Lambada'*   *Paeonia 'Sarah Bernhardt'*   *Origanum vulgare*   *Humulus lupulus*   *Triticum*   *Seasonal produce*

WEDDING AFTERGLOW

THE HEAT OF THE SUN has subsided, leaving guests to enjoy an alfresco dinner on a balmy summer's evening following a perfect country wedding. A memory of the sun stands at the centre of each table: a luscious, golden-orange display of arum lilies (*Zantedeschia*), butterfly weed (*Asclepias*), and galax leaves radiating around a glowing candle, which is protected from the breeze by a glass storm lantern.

Ingredients

Asclepias tuberosa

Zantedeschia elliottiana

Galax urceolata

ARRANGING THE CANDLE

• Fill a 10cm- (4in-) deep, round aluminium tin with soaked, wet foam blocks set onto florist's spikes.
• Sink a candle onto a central prong and place the glass lantern over it.
• Fill the container with water and arrange galax leaves around the glass shield, slightly overlapping them.
• For a warm, golden effect, choose arums in pale yellow, gold, and pale orange.
• Cut each lily stem at a sharp angle and push into the foam around the glass, facing outwards and overlapping the leaves.
• Fill in between the lilies with butterfly weed (*Asclepias tuberosa*) and galax leaves.

SUNFLOWER JAR

SUNFLOWERS AND VAN GOGH are inextricably linked and for this project, which conjures up the breathtaking sunflower fields of southern France, I have chosen a part-glazed jar similar to one in which Van Gogh arranged his famous flowers. As well as the original sunflower (*Helianthus*), with its familiar ruff of bright yellow petals around a rich brown centre, there are now many different varieties: tall and dwarf, single and double, in colours that range from creamy white to orange, red, rust, and chocolate-brown.

PREPARING INGREDIENTS

• If the inside of the jar is not completely glazed, line it with plastic; you could find a watertight container to place inside the jar, but this will need to fit very snugly to remain stable.

• Sunflowers are top-heavy and need to be well anchored; wedge in some soaked wet foam attached to a couple of florist's spikes (*see p.172*). Using a narrow jar will help to keep the sunflowers together.

• Remove most of the leaves from the sunflowers to make them last longer.

• Copper beech leaves (*Fagus sylvatica f. purpurea*) can be used fresh, in summer, when they are purple or when they turn a dark coppery colour in autumn.

• Treat beech leaves (either plain green or copper beech) with glycerine (*see p.182*) before including in a fresh or dried arrangement. To prevent the leaves turning a muddy colour, add some natural dye to the glycerine-water mix.

• Treated beech should not stand in fresh water for more than a week.

Ingredients

Fagus sylvatica f. purpurea

Helianthus annuus

Helianthus annuus 'Autumn Beauty'

SPRING COLOUR IN SUMMER

YELLOW AND BLUE are colours that epitomize spring: golden daffodils and blue skies with scudding white clouds. Summer is full of warmer colours, but it is possible to recapture the fresh feeling that comes at the beginning of the growing season by putting together these spring colours with summer flowers. A strongly textured grey ceramic container makes a simple foil to the clear yellow flowers of spurge (*Euphorbia palustris*) mixed with double blue scabious (*Scabiosa lucida*), love-in-a-mist (*Nigella damascena* Persian Jewel Series), and the intense blue of hound's tongue (*Cynoglossum nervosum*), which all flower at the same time.

FRESH PALETTE

• Flower creations are dictated by what is available; when going to buy flowers, always keep an open mind, perhaps thinking only of a colour palette. The resulting display is often all the more interesting for a touch of improvisation.
• Brilliant blue cornflowers, which are available for most of the year at flower shops, could be substituted for any of the blues used here, and the result would still look fresh and spring-like.

USE THE SETTING

- A narrow trough such as this is ideal for a side table in a hall where there is little space for a more rounded arrangement.
- Consider not only the container but also where it will be displayed. The placing of taller stems towards the ends of this arrangement echoes the upturned ends of the Chinese whatnot below.
- Do not overload your container; this very narrow ceramic trough holds just a single line of flowers.
- It is important to keep small containers topped up with fresh water, particularly if some of the flower stems do not extend to the bottom of the trough.

Euphorbia palustris

Scabiosa lucida

Nigella damascena
Persian Jewel Series

Cynoglossum nervosum

TALL TERRACOTTA POTS

TERRACOTTA POTS WEATHER over the years to give a wonderfully distressed finish. The simplicity and brilliant colours of gerberas seem well suited to these pots, the clusters of daisies just peeping above the rims to make very striking, yet easy to create floor-standing arrangements for a special occasion. Forcers, placed over rhubarb to blanch it to perfection, make fascinating containers for these displays, but long toms are easier to find and can be substituted.

Ingredients

Gerbera jamesonii (red cultivar)

Gerbera jamesonii (gold cultivar)

Gerbera jamesonii (orange cultivar)

Alternative with *pink*

Gerberas have a simple daisy shape that suits all seasons. They are available in flower shops throughout the year in a range of vibrant colours: in spring you could use yellows, cream, and white, in summer gaudy reds and pinks, and for autumn rusty oranges, dark reds, and maroons. Opposing colours can enliven each other (*see pp.10–11*): in the smaller arrangement here, a pleasantly clashing combination of pink and orange gives a bright look. Look out for gerberas with dark centres, as these always stand out beautifully in any arrangement.

USING TERRACOTTA

• As old forcers are open-ended (originally they would have had lids), they need to have containers inside them to hold water.
• Place a brick at the base of each forcer, and stand a container on it with its rim about 5cm (2in) down from the top.
• Unglazed terracotta pots are porous and should be lined.
• The gerberas are cut so that their stems sit on the base of the water container and their heads are held just above rim level.
• Forcers can be used either way up, as long as they can be made stable.

ZINNIA BASKETS

BRIGHT AS BUTTONS and available in a range of vibrant colours, zinnias have appealingly simple, daisy-like flowers, with the added attraction of a ring of tiny yellow starbursts around their central disc. They are such exuberant flowers that we can easily forgive them for being so short-lived; indeed, there is something particularly special about flowers that have a fleeting life. Single roses (*Rosa*), sweet peas (*Lathyrus odoratus*), lily-of-the-valley (*Convallaria majalis*), and gardenias, are all the more marvellous for their transitory life.

Alternative with *dahlias*

The rustic qualities of this simple basket make it equally good for holding a range of other bright, cheerful flowers. The many single or semi-double dahlia cultivars are one possibility: these scarlet-splashed white blooms are especially striking. Dahlias will last for up to a week – and flower well into the autumn in the garden. As with the zinnias, line the basket and wedge in soaked wet foam.

Ingredients

Zinnia elegans

FILLING THE BASKETS

- Find containers to fit inside the baskets or line them with plastic, then wedge in a layer of soaked wet foam.
- Arrange the flowers as if they are growing in the containers, using the bright green leaves to form an attractive layer from which the flowers can spring.
- These baskets give the overall appearance of plants in window boxes and would make a fine display for a window sill.

PUMPKIN DISPLAY

GOURDS LOOK GREAT just as they are: small ones are beautiful, simply piled into a basket and will often last all winter, but they also make extraordinary containers. Here, a medium-sized pumpkin holds chillies (*Capsicum*), pink Japanese anemones, vibrant *Leonotis leonurus*, and lime-green chrysanthemums within an edging of decorative cabbage (*Brassica*). For a perfect Halloween display, set the pumpkin and some candle gourds alongside a turkscap gourd, with its magical combination of glowing orange, green, and white skin and strangely beautiful shape.

FILLING THE GOURDS

- For light holders, remove the tops of small gourds and just enough flesh to fit in a nightlight. Cut the bases of the gourds so that they are level and stable.
- To hollow out a large gourd, cut straight down in a circle around the top. Prise out the top, and scoop out a substantial amount of the flesh. Line with plastic or fit a container inside, wedge in foam, and arrange the flowers.

Ingredients

Capsicum frutescens

Chrysanthemum 'Shamrock'

Anemone x hybrida

Leonotis leonurus

Brassica oleracea 'Tokyo'

SHADES OF GREEN AND LIME

ALL-GREEN ARRANGEMENTS are rare, but green can be every bit as alluring as any of the other colours. It is ever-present in the landscape and is perhaps the most calm and restful of all colours. The fresh green of bells of Ireland (*Moluccella laevis*) and the chartreuse of a *Cymbidium* orchid cultivar are spiced up here by the touch of red of the *Ribes rubrum*, which serves to draw out the subtly different shades. This forward-facing display could be used to fill a disused fireplace.

Ingredients

Moluccella laevis

Allium aflatunense

Ribes rubrum

Cornus alba 'Elegantissima'

Cymbidium Thurso

Alternative with *green*

Removing the chartreuse cymbidium orchids tones down the fresh, spring-like feel of the arrangement and produces a more muted, harmonious combination of shades. Green is on the cool side of the colour wheel (*see pp.10–11*) but the natural tones of the worn copper bowl help to keep the overall feeling here refreshing but not cold.

FILL THE BOWL

• Because this bowl is low and wide, attach florist's prongs inside with adhesive clay and wedge in a low base of soaked wet foam.
• Add the branches of red currant (*Ribes rubrum*) last, so that the fruit is glimpsed through the foliage.
• This all-green arrangement would serve equally well for a special occasion or simply for everyday pleasure.
• Ensure that the bowl is kept topped up with water as this is a thirsty arrangement.
• All the ingredients in this display should last for over a week, but remove individual orchid flowers as they die.

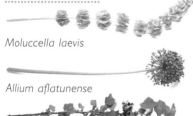

STRIPED FLOWERS

THIS ELEGANT ITALIAN vase has a fluted mouth that makes it easy to arrange flowers in. It may be a little on the large size for everyday use, but it is ideal for a party. In this display, a glorious variety of material – striped flowers in orange, peach, pink, and yellow, together with apricot-coloured berries – cascades outwards.

Ingredients

Ilex verticillata

Hippeastrum 'Masai

Tulipa 'Flaming Parrot

Rosa 'Minuette

PREPARE AND CHOOSE

• Place the largest flowers and stems first to achieve a good balance in the vase.
• The hippeastrums have particularly thick stems: fill them with water before arranging (*see p.178*), to prolong their life.
• Striped, dappled, picoteed, and spotted flowers have long been valued for their distinctive looks. The most interesting examples include carnations and pinks, but there are also camellias, dahlias, ranunculus, zinnias, primulas, and auriculas. Among my favourite striped roses are the red and white 'Roger Lambelin', white and raspberry-pink 'Ferdinand Pichard', and Purple Tiger ('Jacpur'), which is purple and ivory.

SHORELINE CENTREPIECE

A FLOWER ARRANGEMENT is really a still life: each time we create one it is like painting a picture. As shells were often used in seventeenth-century flower paintings, it seems fitting to use them in displays. This beachscape for a dinner party table uses starfish, shells, and hydrangeas; many other flowers and foliage types would suit.

Alternative for a *wooden tray*

A rough wooden tray with rope handles makes an excellent container for a sandy display of shells and sponges but, of course, any collection in such a container must be a dry one. Stop up any holes or cracks in the box with adhesive putty, then fill it to about three-quarters of its depth with silver sand, forming gentle dune-like mounds on which to arrange the shells and sponges. Most of us collect the odd shell and pieces of dead coral from the beach when we are on holiday, although it is worth noting that in some places this is illegal. You may wish to augment your collection with a few special purchases, but marine curios sold in shops are not always sustainably harvested and can include endangered species caught live. Try looking in second-hand shops for sales of old collections.

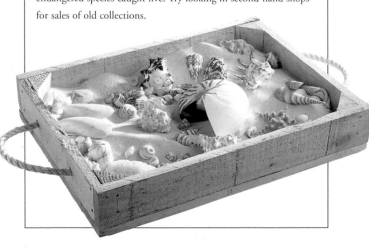

MOULDING THE SHORELINE

• Use a large, plain white ceramic platter – this one is about 40cm x 30cm (16in x 12in) – and make the arrangement in its final position, as the sand shifts if you try to move it.
• Mound silver sand from a builder's merchant in an arc to form a shore, then carefully pour in water.
• Scatter a few shells and starfish in a way that looks good from all angles. Position some of the smaller shells underwater.
• Place the flowers so that their stems are in the water. Sea holly (*Eryngium*) or any coastal plant would look appropriate.

Ingredients

Hydrangea paniculata 'Praecox'

BRIMMING BASKETS

WHEN PLANT arrangements are grouped together, interesting relationships develop between the containers. Here, a picnic basket and a wicker wine carrier are displayed together. Each basket would be fine on its own, but I like the way the smaller one adds depth to the display. The large basket is filled with bittersweet (*Celastrus*), crab apples (*Malus*), and spindle (*Euonymus*), the smaller one with rosehips and bittersweet.

Ingredients

Rosa rugosa hips

Celastrus orbiculatus

Malus x robusta 'Red Sentinel'

Malus 'John Downie'

Euonymus alatus

Ilex verticillata

ARRANGING THE BASKETS

- Line the picnic basket with thick plastic liner and tape up the sides.
- Pack the base of the basket with a layer of soaked, wet foam bricks, then arrange the crab-apple boughs by pushing the stems into the foam. Start with upright branches on the left, with subsequent branches leaning over to the right.
- Place four tumblers of water in the wine container and arrange the rosehip stems in them, making slightly uneven mounds.
- Add some trails of bittersweet – one twisting around the handle and another trailing out at the right-hand corner of the arrangement.

FOIL VASE

THIS DELICATE, elegant glass vase is lined with small pieces of silver foil in patterns of green, black, orange, and bright pink. These colours are echoed in the flowers: the tulips (*Tulipa* 'Estella Rijnveld') have pink stripes and splashes; the berries of the two types of ivy (*Hedera*) are very pronounced and ordered, one green and the other ripening to black; and the silvery broom (*Cytisus*) echoes the silver foil. The flowers are arranged very simply, just springing up and out of the vase, and would be ideally suited to a glass or metal shelf.

Ingredients

Cytisus multiflorus

Tulipa 'Estella Rijnveld'

Hedera canariensis 'Gloire de Marengo'

Hedera helix f. poetarum 'Poetica Arborea'

Alternative with *fritillaries*

Nodding snakeskin fritillaries (*Fritillaria meleagris*) in plum and white match the foil vase perfectly. Although these incredible flowers look fragile, they should last up to six days if they are bought just as they are opening (*see p.176*).

PRACTICAL POINTS

• Vases with decoration on the inside, such as this, need a watertight lining or inner container to protect them.

• The tulips will continue to grow in the vase and, although they may need to be cut back a little if they get too straggly, the sinuous curves into which their stems evolve are often most attractive.

• The vase life of many flowers can be shortened by the presence of tulips in the same arrangement, but this combination should last reasonably well.

EARLY SUMMER SKIES

THE BRIDGE BETWEEN spring and summer is one of the most beautiful times of the floral year: plants are fresh and sparkling, their colours enhanced by the early summer skies. Among the beauties that flower at this time are Solomon's seal (*Polygonatum*) and snowball bush (*Viburnum macrocephalum*) – both white with green undertones – which I have added to some early, pale blue delphiniums in this etched glass vase. The blue backdrop intensifies the theme, but these flowers would look equally attractive against a green, yellow, or white background.

CHOOSING A VASE

• A conical vase always makes for simple, attractive arrangements: the bottom and rim hold the first few stems securely in place, making management of the rest of the arrangement easier, while the shape allows flowers and foliage to spring outwards in a beautifully natural way.

• Ensure that the stems of the Solomon's seal (Polygonatum) curve outwards, so that their demure little white and green flowers can be easily seen.

• To prolong the life of the flowers on the snowball bush, remove most of the lower leaves from the stems before arranging them in the vase. This will also help to prevent the display from looking too leafy.

Ingredients

Viburnum macrocephalum

Delphinium 'Lord Butler'

BAMBOO TRIPOD

THIS STRIKINGLY SIMPLE arrangement is reminiscent of a Japanese water garden. A graceful bamboo tripod supports a dark copper-glazed bowl containing a floating amber-coloured chrysanthemum and pine twigs (*Pinus nigra*). Standing beside it, a larger, similar bowl echoes the composition of the first. The scale of the tripod and bowl can be adjusted, and the plant material can be varied to suit the season.

CREATING THE DESIGN

- To create the tripod for a bowl that is about 25cm (10in) in diameter, you will need three bamboo canes measuring 1.5cm (½in) across and 43cm (17in) long.
- With a small saw, cut one end of each bamboo cane at an angle, cutting at a joint to prevent the bamboo splintering. Cut the other end of each cane straight across.
- Tie the canes together with mossing wire, 20cm (8in) from the bottom, with the angled ends upwards, and form a stable base. Splay the canes out so that each one is at right angles to the others,

then bind them securely in position.
- Paint the bamboo to suit the bowl and location: I sprayed this tripod with cranberry-coloured paint, applied a light coat of gold, then highlighted the joints with more cranberry.
- Bind the joint with ribbon to conceal the wire.
- Choose flowers that will float and last well in water, such as chrysanthemums, roses, begonias, camellias, dahlias, and anemones.

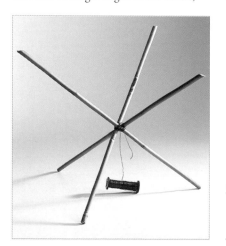

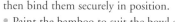

Ingredients

Pinus nigra

Chrysanthemum 'Tom Pearce'

FLOWERS UNDER WATER

Rosa 'Blue Curiosa'

Allium giganteum

Eustoma grandiflorum Heidi Series

Eustoma grandiflorum Heidi Series

Paeonia 'Red Charm'

Nigella damascena var.

APPEARING TO FLOAT in space, flower heads of rose, peony, eustoma, love-in-a-mist (*Nigella damascena var.*), and decorative onion (*Allium giganteum*) are here magnified and reflected underwater by an inverted pyramid of glass tumblers.

CREATING THE DISPLAY

• Decide how long you need the display to last. If longevity is required, omit the onion, which, although it looks superb, will cloud the water in a couple of days.

• Find a large "fish-bowl" vase, about 35cm (14in) tall, into which you can fit 10 or 11 tumblers, preferably ridged rather than plain to add to the refraction of light.

• Fill the vase with water to just over three-quarters of its capacity.

• Cut off the stems just below the flower

heads and place one bloom inside each tumbler, facing towards the rim.

• Top up the tumblers with water.

• Invert the tumblers under the surface of the vase water, with their rims facing outwards. Begin by wedging in the first three at the bottom, each one facing down at 45°, then pile on the others, positioning the flowers as you work.

• Float a selection of the remaining flowers on the surface of the water.

VIVID BLUES

INSPIRATION FOR THIS DISPLAY was provided by the intense colours of the matt glazes on this conical vase. The forget-me-nots (*Myosotis sylvatica*) are beautiful in the detail of their clear sky-blue flowers, while the blue of the willow gentian (*Gentiana asclepiadea*) is rich and warm. Such a simple arrangement would particularly suit a contemporary setting – maybe on a glass, stone, or metal side table. It would last well on a table outside, but should be brought in if frost is forecast.

CHOOSING INGREDIENTS

• In many places, larch twigs (Larix decidua) are available during winter, when such fresh-looking greenery is scarce. The twigs can be kept in water in a cool place outside when other material in the arrangement has faded; they will last for several months and can be used again.

• The flowers of forget-me-nots are not long lasting once cut, but in a coolish temperature, especially outside or in a porch where they can be admired as you go in and out of the house, they should look good for about five days. As their fleshy stems are not very long it will be important to keep the vase topped up so that the shorter stems stay below the water.

• Gentians carry some of the bluest flowers of all and the willow gentian is no exception. Although summer-flowering, willow gentians are available all year from florists. For best results, remove most of their leaves, as well as any fading flowers.

Alternative with *viburnum*

A much cooler and more serene arrangement can be created by replacing the vibrant blue willow gentians with the superb greeny white flowers of snowball bush (*Viburnum macrocephalum*). Most of the leaves of the viburnum have been removed: this not only makes the flower heads last longer but gives a cleaner look to the display. Because of the delicate forget-me-nots, this design will also last best outside in cool temperatures.

Ingredients

Larix decidua

Gentiana asclepiadea

Myosotis sylvatica 'Music'

FRESH GREEN AND WHITE

SIMPLICITY OF LINE and colour defines this display. Tall, elegant, pure white lilies and delphiniums, exotic emerald arums (*Zantedeschia aethiopica* 'Green Goddess') and anthuriums, and fresh green larch (*Larix decidua*) branches are arrayed in a large, hand-built pot with a lichen-like finish. The delphiniums were chosen because their near-black centres stand out so well. Place vases on either side of the altar or use them as an imposing floor-standing arrangement at a reception.

USING LILIES

• Madonna lilies (*Lilium candidum*) can be found for only a limited period, but *L. longiflorum* is available all year round in flower shops and can be substituted.

• Lilies are noted for their scent, but this varies from one kind to another: Madonna lilies have a very sweet fragrance, while others have a more spicy note, and some are even unpleasant.

• Be sure to remove the flowers' pollen anthers if they are likely to be brushed up against: lilies have strongly coloured yellow pollen that stains fabric immediately. As the flower buds open and before the pollen develops, grasp all the anthers and gently pull them towards you: they will easily become detached from their green stamen filaments. Leave the central stigma intact.

• All these cut flowers, but especially the lilies, take up copious amounts of water.

Ingredients

Anthurium 'Midori'

Delphinium 'Sandpiper'

Lilium candidum

Zantedeschia aethiopica 'Green Goddess'

Larix decidua

Alternative with *foxgloves*

Foxgloves (*Digitalis*) are at the height of their flowering season at the same time of year as Madonna lilies. There are pure white foxglove cultivars that would look ravishing with the other white flowers used in the main arrangement, but to give the arrangement a different, more countrified feel, include a few spires of the more familiar pink foxgloves with purple-spotted throats. These also relate well to the finish of the vase.

PERFUMED PUNCHBOWL

TWO COUNTRY GARDEN PLANTS are used in this display: mignonette (*Reseda odorata*) and an English marigold (*Calendula officinalis*). The toasted colour of the marigold works well with the orange anthers of the mignonette, while a glass bowl shows off the slim stalks. This informal centrepiece will perfume any room with its mix of scents.

MAINTAIN THE DISPLAY

• Remove all the leaves from the stems of the mignonette: this is a fiddly job but, as they rot extremely quickly, it is worth doing.
• Change the water every day. The flowers are closely arranged so it is quite easy to hold them with a hand just inside the bowl and tip the water away. Replace with water that has a few drops of bleach in it.
• Mignonette has a tantalizing scent that resembles a blend of violets, fresh hay and sweet peas. Unlike most other flowers, the blooms retain much of this perfume even

when they are dried, so it is worth preserving them when this arrangement is past its best. Simply snip off the flower heads and put them in a bowl with some other flower petals to dry: they will continue to release their perfume for many weeks.
• In the garden both marigolds and mignonettes grow readily from seed. Although the mignonette is not showy, it rewards with its delectable perfume. The marigolds help to keep aphids at bay.

Alternative with *orchids*

A slightly wilder and more exotic display can be created by replacing the marigolds with one of the more delicate-looking orchids – here the little yellow blooms of the *Dendrobium* cultivar 'Golden Showers'. In this arrangement, the mignonette makes a low, tussocky surface close to the bowl, which is punctuated by the stems of orchids rising up out of the bowl and spraying outwards and down over the mignonette flowers.

Ingredients

Reseda odorata

Calendula officinalis
'Indian Prince'

TROPICAL ANEMONES

Ingredients

Anemone coronaria De Caen Group

Areca lutescens

THESE BRILLIANT RED anemones (*Anemone coronaria* De Caen Group) and fronds of areca palm (*Chrysalidocarpus lutescens*) look very elegant in their three glass vases, perhaps adorning a side table in a hall or living room. Anemones are naturally at their best in spring, but they can be found all year round in a range of stunningly intense colours.

ARRANGING THE ANEMONES

• Fill three glass vases with water and group them in an interesting and pleasing way. The vases could be identical or you may prefer to mix shapes.
• Arrange palm foliage in all three vases, aiming for a striking, full effect but without cramming in too many leaves.
• Shorten the stems of three or four anemone blooms, and submerge them at varying depths in the vases, taking care not to damage or fold the petals when pushing the blooms between the palm stems.
• Complete the display by carefully adding the upright anemone stems.

Alternative with *orchids*

Using the same three vases and palm foliage, you can create a softer, more diffuse effect by substituting yellow-flowered orchids, such as these *Oncidium flexuosum*. The feathery plumes last very well, but they are too small to be submerged in the water, as was done with the anemones in the original display.

FRAMED CENTREPIECE

WHILE CHANGING the frame of a painting one day, I thought that the frame could work as a table centrepiece with flowers and fruits arranged within it. It would last only a few hours – but long enough for a dinner party. Within the frame, on a bed of ferns, are roses (*Rosa* Dutch Gold®), yellow mariposa (*Calochortus luteus*), and some glistening red currants.

Ingredients

Red currants

Rosa Dutch Gold®

Polystichum setiferum

Calochortus luteus

MAKING THE CENTREPIECE

- Choose a frame that complements the colours of the ingredients you plan to use.
- Stick a piece of black or dark green card to the back of the frame so that you can move the arrangement once it is done.
- Cover the card with a bed of fern leaves, allowing tips to stray out onto the frame.
- Twist the petals off two roses to reveal their decorative calyces; place the whole rose, the calyces, and the loose petals on the ferns, along with the mariposa flowers.
- Fill in between the flowers, petals, and fern leaves with clusters of red currants.

Alternative with *ivy*

A gilt picture frame has been used here to give a more ornate, Italianate look. The base layer is a delicate ivy (*Hedera nepalensis* 'Suzanne') on which are arranged campanula flowers, a eustoma (*Eustoma grandiflorum*) flower and petals, *Nectaroscordum siculum*, and pale pink *Lamium maculatum*. Luscious blueberries fill in the background.

EXOTIC BASKET

A WOVEN PLASTIC shopping basket in gaudy hues is the humorous inspiration for this vivid arrangement. The hot colours of the basket have a South American or Mexican feel, so the sunny, papery flowers of satin flower or godetia (*Clarkia amoena*), which is native to those regions, seemed appropriate. Their salmon and fuchsia pinks clash deliciously with the orange of the blood flower (*Asclepias curassavica*), which is also of South American origin. To achieve the best result, it is vital not to lose your nerve with the colours: think hot, hot, hot.

USING PLASTIC BASKETS

- Place a brick in the base of baskets such as these to ensure stability.
- Line the basket with plastic, and wedge in soaked wet foam to about 5cm (2in) below the rim.
- Arrange the flowers standing straight up, to look as if they are almost growing out of the basket.
- Snip off the individual godetia flowers as they fade: this will encourage more buds to open further up the stem.
- Check and top up the water in the display frequently.

Ingredients

Asclepias curassavica

Clarkia amoena Grace Series

Clarkia amoena Grace Series

Clarkia amoena Grace Series

Clarkia amoena
Grace Series

Alternative with *celosia*

For another, slightly darker, combination, use bright crimson satin flowers, bright orange blood flowers, and some brilliant scarlet cockscombs (*Celosia argentea* Century Series). Remove most of the leaves from the cockscombs, as they have a tendency to droop.

DRAMATIC SPRING FLOWERS

Camellia japonica 'Elegans'

SPRING GIVES US not only soft pastels, but also much more intensely coloured flowers. The cultivars of tulips (*Tulipa*), anemones, and camellias all have a plentiful supply of particularly rich colours. Here, scarlet tulips with a black blotch at the base of each petal combine with purple De Caen anemones and warm, bright pink camellias in a dramatic display to brighten a living room or garden table.

Anemone coronaria De Caen Group

Tulipa 'Exotic Bird'

Alternative with *orange*

The red of the tulips, so lively when offset against the purple anemones in the main display, appears more mellow when they are combined with orange chincherinchees (*Ornithogalum dubium*) and fritillaries. This is because scarlet and orange are close to each other on the colour wheel (*see pp.10–11*), lying on the warm side between yellow and red. The overall effect is still an invigorating mix but it is much easier on the eye.

MAKE IT LAST

• Always buy anemones in bud, when they are just beginning to show colour (*see p.176*); they will last well once they have been conditioned (*see pp.176–179*).

• All flowers have a longer vase life in cool places but this is particularly the case with tulips. The arrangement would last longest if kept outdoors in a spot where it could be seen from the living room or kitchen. Cool winter weather should give the tulips a vase life of 21 days; however, very hard frost would destroy the flowers.

• Remove flowers from the stems of the camellia as they fade to encourage more buds to open.

• This glass-lined wire vase is an excellent shape in which to display flowers.

CHRISTMAS SHOPPING

THE BRILLIANT orange-red of a felt shopping bag complements to perfection this spectacular winter display. Rich, dark green holly (*Ilex*) and magnificent red stems of dogwood tower above the rim of anthuriums (*Anthurium veitchii*), whose ivory spathes darken to red at their edges, while their jaunty spadices almost match the colour of the basket.

PREPARING THE BASKET

- Having chosen a suitable bag or basket for your arrangement, find a bucket or watertight container to fit inside it.
- Stuff rolled newspaper around the base of the bucket; this will help to support the bag or basket and give it a good shape.

- Wedge a block of soaked wet foam at the base of the bucket to help keep the stems in position, especially when you are beginning to create the display.
- First place the dogwood twigs, slightly taller in the centre than at the sides.

Next, arrange the holly, aiming to create a three-dimensional arrangement. Finally, add the anthuriums around the rim, taking care not to make them too even.
- Top up the water as necessary, adding a few drops of bleach each time.

Ingredients

Ilex x meserveae 'Blue Prince'

Cornus alba 'Sibirica'

Anthurium andraeanum 'Fantasia'

Alternative with *hydrangea*

Not as startling in their effect as the anthuriums, the *Hydrangea macrophylla* are none the less an attractive alternative with their green-tinged red, mauve, and pink flowers. Whereas I simply edged the bag with the anthuriums, I have mounded the hydrangea flowers from the front to the back of the bag. They will dry on the stem and the display will last for several weeks provided the dogwood and holly stems are in water.

GLASS CYLINDERS

THIS STUNNING EFFECT is achieved by sandwiching yellow and orange lentils between two closely fitting glass cylinders. Erupting out of them are flowers in a close range of slightly clashing, piquant colours full of life and sunshine: cockscombs (*Celosia*), snapdragons (*Antirrhinum*), red hot pokers (*Kniphofia*), and blanket flowers (*Gaillardia*). These shades of orange, apricot-pink, and carmine are particularly vibrant when used together: the leanings towards both blue and yellow produce excitement. Although creating this effect takes a little longer than using a simple vase, the finished result is well worth the effort.

Ingredients

Gaillardia x grandiflora 'Burgunder'

Antirrhinum majus Coronette Series

Kniphofia 'C.M. Prichard'

Celosia argentea Olympia Series

FILLING THE CONTAINERS

• Find two glass cylinders, one of which will fit inside the other, leaving a gap of approximately 1cm (½in).
• Fill the smaller of the two cylinders wit water to 3.5cm (1½in) from the rim.
• Place a small piece of florist's adhesive clay on the bottom of the smaller cylinde

...nd push it down into the larger vase.
...Using a funnel, pour lentils between
...e two glasses. Make a simple pattern by
...oving the funnel around as you feed two
...olours of lentils into it.
...To help these flowers last a week, add
... few drops of bleach to the water and
...move fading snapdragon blooms.

EASTER NEST

A MOSSY NEST filled with eggs and sweet-scented spring flowers makes a very special Easter gift. Surrounding the little pile of blue hen's eggs are flowers in soft pastel shades, including white and pink hyacinths (*Hyacinthus orientalis* 'White Pearl' and 'Lady Derby'), the narcissus cultivar 'Cragford', pale pink Persian buttercups (*Ranunculus asiaticus* Turban Group), ornamental cabbage (*Brassica oleracea*), Christmas roses (*Helleborus niger*), and golden-yellow polyanthus (*Primula*).

ARRANGING THE NEST

- Find an oval plastic container deep enough to hold and conceal soaked wet foam, and large enough to accommodate the eggs and all the flower stems.
- Using chicken wire, construct a firm, oval base for the container to sit on.
- Make a chicken-wire tube and fill it with sphagnum moss; the tube must be long enough to form into a ring around the container and the chicken-wire base. Attach the ring to the base with wire.
- Attach enough carpet moss and reindeer moss to completely cover the outside of the chicken-wire and moss ring.
- Fill the container with soaked wet foam.
- Place the eggs in a pile, on the foam, slightly off-centre.
- Arrange the flowers in the soaked wet foam, placing the taller ones in groups at the back of the container. Fill in between the flowers and the eggs with a layer of moss.

Alternative with *yellows*

In this sunny alternative, the pink hyacinths and ranunculus have been omitted, and only yellow, cream, and white flowers are used. There are creamy yellow hyacinths, as well as the white ones, and white narcissus. Sprigs of fragrant yellow mimosa (*Acacia*) add to the delicious spring scents of the display.

Ingredients

Reindeer moss

Sphagnum moss

Hedera

Narcissus 'Cragford'

Hyacinthus orientalis 'White Pearl'

Hyacinthus orientalis 'Lady Derby'

Ranunculus asiaticus Turban Group

Brassica oleracea

Helleborus niger

Primula Polyanthus Group

TRAILING LILIES

THE BEAUTY of these climbing lilies is breathtaking. Natives of the tropics, they are available for most of the year. The flowers of the most usually seen gloriosa lily have brilliant scarlet petals with yellow edgings and a lime-green base; the petals furl back and the ends of the leaves narrow to act as tendrils. Here the natural twining shape is used to hang down as well as to spray out of the basket, making a perfect display for either a low table or a wide window sill. The lilies are complemented by the spiky looking flowers of *Centaurea montana* (a blue knapweed) and a scarlet cultivar of *Monarda* (bergamot or bee balm).

Ingredients

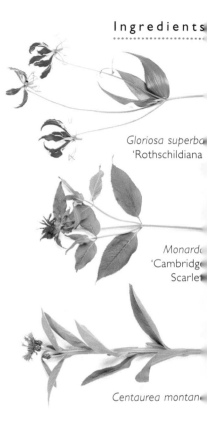

Gloriosa superba 'Rothschildiana

Monarda 'Cambridge Scarlet

Centaurea montana

PRACTICAL POINTS

• Always try to find a well-fitting, watertight container to fit inside any basket used in an arrangement. Plastic sheeting can be used, but it may be pierced by the stalks of any woody stemmed flowers or foliage used in the arrangement, or even by the wicker itself.

• Gloriosa lilies have one drawback: all parts of the plant are extremely poisonous, so do not under any circumstances use their petals as food decoration.

• Bergamot is so named because its scent is similar to that of the bergamot (*Citrus bergamia*) used in Earl Grey tea: rub the petals occasionally to release the fragrance.

Alternative with *red and green*

The main arrangement is softened by the blue flowers. Remove them and the display becomes more potent, with a vibrant feel. The flowers of *Monarda* 'Cambridge Scarlet' have a green base and thin scarlet petals, and both leaves and flowers are aromatic. The wicker basket, with its warm red-brown tones, relates well to the reds of the flowers.

VIBRANT ANEMONES

COLOURS THAT LIE ADJACENT or close to each other on the colour wheel (*see pp.10–11*) mostly harmonize, although bluey purple and orangey red can react quite vibrantly. Here, rich purple anemones (*Anemone coronaria* De Caen Group) and liatris (*Liatris spicata*), which is on the blue side of red, vie with orange-red ranunculus (*Ranunculus asiaticus*) (on the yellow side of red); these in turn sing out against the green anemone leaf bracts and stalks. Set against a rich Venetian red background, all this makes for an exciting display that revels in colour while the arrangement itself has been kept deliberately simple in form.

Alternative with *yellow*

Here the same rectangular glass vase and similarly shaped flowers are used to quite different effect. Harmonizing yellows, ranging from a rich egg-yolk yellow, through gold, to greeny yellow and cream, give a bright, sunny arrangement. Again, just three types of flower are used: golden rod (*Solidago*), Iceland poppies (*Papaver nudicaule*), and eustoma.

Ingredients

Anemone coronaria
De Caen Group

Ranunculus asiaticus
Turban Group

Liatris spicata

ARRANGE THE FLOWERS

• Although it looks simple, this kind of arrangement requires care to create.
• Start by propping some of the shorter flower stems almost vertically against the left side of the vase.
• Add more stems, allowing them to spra out gently; the first stems will help to hol them in place.
• The stems leaning out to the right of th vase should be the longest, so that the ends of their stems reach the bottom of the left side and hold them in place.

If our plant materials are to realize

their peak potential, we need to treat

them with care and consideration.

Lasting quality is achieved by simple

conditioning, which is explained in

PRACTICAL TECHNIQUES

this section. Here, too, are techniques

for wiring – useful to achieve a desired

shape – and ways to preserve plant

material for quietly glowing displays

of unique beauty.

TOOLS AND EQUIPMENT

UNLIKE MANY CRAFTS that demand the acquisition of expensive pieces of equipment before you can get started, arranging flowers requires very few tools. In fact the simpler projects often require little more than a pair of florist's scissors and some wet or dry foam. If you decide to try some of the slightly more advanced projects, then the other tools and props illustrated below may prove useful. Flowers and containers are your main ingredients, of course, and having a good supply of vases to choose from will be your greatest asset. Before starting a project, always make sure that everything you need is at hand.

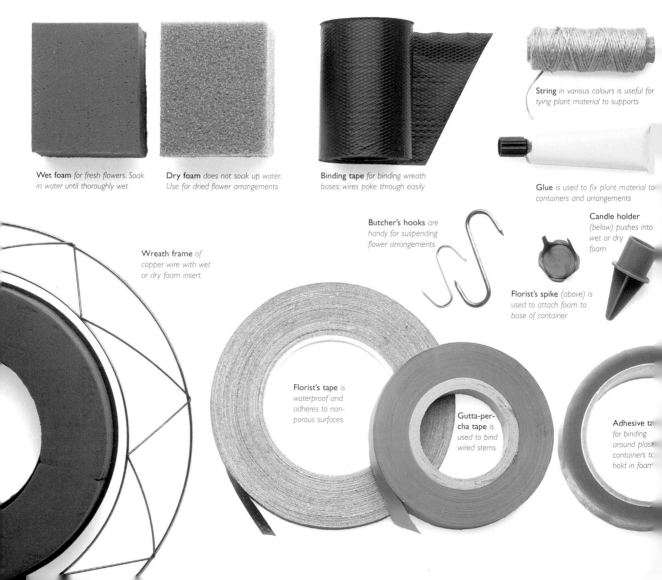

Wet foam *for fresh flowers. Soak in water until thoroughly wet*

Dry foam *does not soak up water. Use for dried flower arrangements*

Binding tape *for binding wreath bases; wires poke through easily*

String *in various colours is useful for tying plant material to supports*

Glue *is used to fix plant material to containers and arrangements*

Wreath frame *of copper wire with wet or dry foam insert*

Butcher's hooks *are handy for suspending flower arrangements*

Candle holder *(below) pushes into wet or dry foam*

Florist's spike *(above) is used to attach foam to base of container*

Florist's tape *is waterproof and adheres to non-porous surfaces*

Gutta-per-cha tape *is used to bind wired stems*

Adhesive ta *for binding around plast containers to hold in foam*

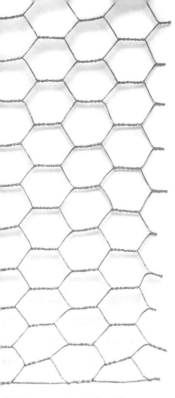

Chicken wire *can be bought in 2.5cm (1in) and 1.25cm (½in) gauges*

Rose wire *is fine silver wire for wedding work*

Reel wire *is used for fine work such as wiring single flowers to stub wires*

Thin-gauge stub wires *are ideal for wiring small single flowers and leaves*

Medium-gauge stub wire *is used for wiring medium-weight material*

Heavy-gauge stub wires *are needed for wiring larger flower heads and plant material*

Florist's scissors *are useful for cutting stems and removing leaves and thorns*

Carpet moss *provides useful background material*

Secateurs *are essential for cutting heavier woody stems*

Sphagnum moss *is used for filling chicken-wire bases*

A pruning knife *is handy for cutting and scraping stems*

Glue gun and glue sticks *provide a neat method of attaching materials to containers. Cool-melt models are safest to use but hot-melt is stronger*

Spanish moss *is available dyed (left) or natural (right)*

Bun moss *can be used fresh and preserved*

Wire cutters *are used to cut stub wires and chicken wire*

CONTAINERS

AN ESSENTIAL REQUIREMENT in the flower arranger's store cupboard is a few basic, well-shaped containers. Vases with rectangular or trumpet profiles are the easiest to use, as these shapes hold flowers without the need for foam, pinholder, or wire support. For everyday use, I find that glass containers are the most adaptable; a group of three rectangular glass vases can be used either singly or in combination, according to how many flowers you are displaying and how large your display area may be.

TYPES OF CONTAINER

Glass, metal, ceramic, terracotta, stone, and basketware receptacles have long been the traditional containers in which to display flowers, but I like to use a variety of "found" objects, such as old boxes, saucepans, kettles, cups, and drinking glasses, as well as conventional vases. What you should always look for are containers that work together with the flowers to produce arrangements that look both natural and inevitable. Of course, practicality must also be borne in mind: stone, for example, can be heavy to move, while containers that require plastic liners – such as those made of wicker and terracotta – could possibly spring a leak and damage a valuable piece of furniture.

GLASS provides an extremely sympathetic material for vases, and I love to see flower stems in clear glass vases. As glassware surfaces are shiny, however, the material is less appropriate for rustic arrangements.

METAL containers, such as those made of brass, copper, bronze, pewter, aluminium, iron, and lead, work particularly well for larger displays. However, small silver or copper beakers and jugs also make elegant receptacles.

TERRACOTTA, with its warm, earthy look, is ideal for rustic arrangements. One of my favourite materials is weather-distressed terracotta, when salts have leached through the surface and moss has taken hold.

CERAMIC is, along with glass, the most popular medium for vases. Stoneware can carry exceptionally beautiful glazes, but the lower fired, more porous pieces need to be well glazed to prevent them leaking.

BASKETWORK containers made of wicker, vine, and twigs are the most rustic of all containers. If you are using them for fresh flowers, they must be lined with either a rigid or flexible plastic liner (*see p.308*).

ADAPTING CONTAINERS

INCREASING HEIGHT

Flower stems do not always come in just
the lengths that we require, which may be
a problem when creating large-scale projects
or using deep containers. As an alternative
to using flower funnels (*right*) when longer
lengths are required, I sometimes
improvise by using the tubes that orchids
come in, pushing a stem into a tube filled
with water, then attaching the tube plus
flower to a strong stem or stick higher up
in the arrangement. An alternative to
raising the inner base of a deep container
(*below*) is to increase the length of stems by
wiring them to stub wires (*see pp.184-
185*). This was done with the violets on
pp.76–77, to charming effect. These last
two methods are, of course, only possible
when the container being used is opaque
rather than translucent.

FLOWER FUNNELS can be pushed straight into
the soaked wet foam in which you are arranging
flowers or, if you need even more height, they
can be wired to lengths of bamboo inserted into
the arrangement. Render the funnels invisible
by smothering them in foliage

RAISE THE BASE of a deep container, such as the rhubarb forcer shown
here, by placing two bricks inside it, then placing a vase on top of the
bricks so that its rim comes to just below the rim of the outer container.
This reduces the length of flower required by some 23–25cm (9–10in).

PICKING AND CONDITIONING

Whether you buy your flowers from a flower shop or stall or pick them from your own garden, the same basic rules of selection and conditioning apply. To get the longest possible life out of the flowers that you use, they need to be carefully chosen in the first place and then well conditioned. Conditioning takes a little extra time, but it can make an enormous difference to the life of a flower. Different types of flower require different conditioning techniques, and these are described in the following pages.

CHOOSING FLOWERS

When buying flowers, choose those with healthy leaves and flowers that are in bud and just beginning to open. If the flowers are too tightly budded, they may never open, and if they are too open they will perish quickly. Buy flowers from a reliable vendor who restocks frequently and keeps the flowers in good condition. If gathering flowers from your own garden, choose them in the same way and avoid picking them in the heat of the day.

Fully open flower

TOO EARLY
The flower is not showing colour and the tight leaf sheath may dry together with the bud and stop it opening. Draw back the sheath to help prevent this.

JUST RIGHT
The flower bud is just beginning to show colour and it should open perfectly. Choose flowers in this condition for the healthiest and longest lasting flower arrangements.

TOO LATE
The flower is fully open and is fine if you want it to look perfect on the day you buy or pick it. However, it will not last as long as the just-opening bud of the middle example.

HOW TO CONDITION FLOWERS

GREEN-STEMMED FLOWERS

All green-stemmed flowers must have their lower leaves
removed, as any leaves that are submerged in water will
rot easily, dramatically shortening the life of a flower.
Then, bearing in mind the size of your arrangement,
trim the flower stems: the shorter the stem, the longer
the flower will last.

1 REMOVE 5cm (2in)
of stem from long
flower stems, cutting at
the sharpest possible
angle. With short-
stemmed flowers,
remove as much stem
as possible, bearing in
mind the size of your
arrangement.

*Remove all
lower leaves*

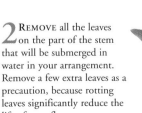

2 REMOVE all the leaves
on the part of the stem
that will be submerged in
water in your arrangement.
Remove a few extra leaves as a
precaution, because rotting
leaves significantly reduce the
life of your flowers.

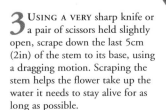

3 USING A VERY sharp knife or
a pair of scissors held slightly
open, scrape down the last 5cm
(2in) of the stem to its base, using
a dragging motion. Scraping the
stem helps the flower take up the
water it needs to stay alive for as
long as possible.

WOODY STEMS

The branches of flowering shrubs such as lilac and mock orange (as well as of much foliage) have woody stems that take up water with difficulty. To assist the process, remove the lower leaves from each stem and cut the end at a sharp angle. Hammer about 2.5cm (1in) of the stem end and scrape the stems a little above the crushed sections. This will help to increase the surface area for water uptake.

MILKY SAPPED STEMS

Flowers such as milkweed, spurge, and poppies, whose stems contain milky sap, are best heat-sealed before arranging in water. After removing the lower leaves, cut straight across the stems with a sharp knife and hold the bottom 2.5cm (1in) in a flame until it starts to burn. Do not cut the stems again after burning – the flowers are now ready to be arranged in water.

HOLLOW STEMS

Some flowers, such as amaryllis, lupin, delphinium, and arum lily, have large, hollow stems that can be filled with water to help them last longer in arrangements. Once the stems are filled and plugged, leave them to stand in a bucket of water to take up water in the usual way. As an alternative to plugging the stem with cotton wool, after filling with water, place your thumb over the end and upend the stem into a vase filled with water.

1 HOLD THE FLOWER upside down and fill the hollow stem with cold water. Note that the stem has been cut at an angle to create a larger surface area for water uptake.

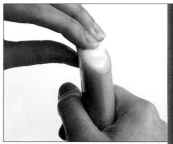

2 SEAL THE STEM with a moist cotton-wool plug to keep the water in and still allow water uptake once the flowers have been arranged.

STRAIGHTENING TULIP STEMS

It is possible to improve the condition of forced tulips, whose weak stems often droop in an awkward way. Remove some of the leaves, then cut the stems at an angle with a sharp knife. Make a vertical slit in the stem to further increase the area capable of taking up water, then follow the techniques described below.

PRICK THE STEM
If tulips have been out of water for some time, air may have become trapped in the stems, preventing water uptake and causing the flowers to wilt prematurely. To release trapped air, carefully prick the stem of each tulip with a fine, sterilized needle just below the flower head.

1 AFTER PREPARING THE STEMS, wrap the tulips in waxed florist's tissue, which will retain its rigidity in water. Alternatively, use brown paper or newspaper.

2 STAND THE TULIPS in cold water for several hours. To assist the straightening process and to strengthen the stems, add florist's conditioning powder to the water.

HOT WATER TREATMENT

To counteract drooping, place the prepared flowers in a deep, supportive holder containing about 5cm (2in) of very hot (not quite boiling) water. Leave for five minutes then top up with cold water. Allow the flowers to recover before arranging them.

REMOVING POLLEN

Many lilies carry pollen that can stain heavily. Although they look best with their pollen intact, it is wise to remove it, especially if the flowers are to be placed in a position where someone could brush against them. It is best to remove pollen before it develops as it is easy then to grasp all the stamens between two fingers and pull off the pollen sacs in one go.

COLD WATER TREATMENT

It is sensible to prepare all flowers before embarking on any arrangements. Simple measures, such as adding conditioning powder to vase water or refreshing flowers in deep, cool water, may add considerably to the longevity of your arrangements.

CONDITIONING POWDER
To revive drooping blooms, wrap the flower heads in paper, stand the flowers in warm water, and add florist's conditioning powder. Leave for several hours while the warm water eliminates air locks.

MAINTAINING FRESHNESS
Place flowers that are ready to use in a bucket or other large container part-filled with cool water. Leave for two hours or so before beginning an arrangement.

PRESERVING MATERIAL

PRESERVED FLOWERS and leaves have a unique, muted beauty that is reminiscent of the colours in old tapestries. Use their unique qualities to create quietly glowing creations, rather than trying to emulate fresh flower arrangements. Do resist the temptation to keep preserved flower arrangements for too long: after three months, light exposure causes them to lose their colour and they will begin to look tired and dusty. Of the three methods of preserving plant material that are described here, air drying is the easiest and, I think, the most successful.

AIR DRYING

DRYING IN A VASE

Many flowers will air dry if simply left to stand in a vase. After conditioning the flowers (*see pp.176–177*), place them in a vase filled with about 2.5cm (1in) of water and leave them while the water dries out. Baby's breath, sea thistle, globe thistle, yarrow, strawflower, larkspur, grasses, and beech leaves are all suitable for this drying method. Roses and delphiniums dry this way too – as I find sometimes by default. Although air drying plant material in a vase is not as effective as hanging bunches up to dry, it is a simple technique and can be successful with the right flowers.

Good Air-drying Material   V=Vase H=Hang

Acanthus (Bear's breeches)	V/H	*Fagus* (Beech)	V/H
Achillea (Yarrow)	V/H	*Gypsophila* (Baby's breath)	V/H
Allium (Onion)	V/H	*Lavandula* (Lavender)	H
Astilbe (Astilbe)	H	*Moluccella* (Bells of Ireland)	H
Calendula (Marigold)	H	*Monarda* (Bergamot)	H
Centaurea cyanus (Cornflower)	H	*Nigella* (Love-in-a-mist)	V/H
Consolida (Larkspur)	V/H	*Paeonia* (Peony)	H
Cortaderia (Pampas grass)	H	*Physalis* (Chinese lanterns)	V/H
Delphinium (Delphinium)	H	*Rosa* (Rose)	H
Echinops (Globe thistle)	V/H	*Salvia viridis* (Clary sage)	H
Eryngium (Sea thistle)	V/H	*Solidago* (Golden rod)	V/H

HANGING BUNCHES

This very effective method of air drying requires a coolish, dry, airy, dark place, such as an airing cupboard or cellar, in which to hang the bunches while they slowly dry. The best time to pick flowers for drying is late morning on a dry day.

1 REMOVE ALL LOWER leaves from the flowers as squashed leaves will lead to rotting, which will ruin your dried flowers. Flowers need to be just opening, in good condition, and with dry stems.

2 TIE SMALL BUNCHES of the flowers together, making sure that they are not rubbing against each other and that there are no leaves caught in the tie. Leave a long length of string free to hang up the bunches.

3 CHOOSE A SUITABLE drying place and hang the bunches from a rail so that they do not touch. Leave for between one and three weeks until the flowers are thoroughly dry.

OTHER TECHNIQUES

PRESERVING PLANTS WITH GLYCERINE

Many flowers can be preserved using glycerine, but the best results are obtained with foliage. Condition the material (*see pp. 176–177*), then place it in a large container in a solution of 40 per cent glycerine to 60 per cent hot water. When beads of glycerine show on the flowers or leaves, the material is ready. Plants tend to lose colour when preserved; to remedy this, add some natural dye to the solution, matching the colour of the flowers or leaves.

Good Plants for Glycerine

Acer (Maple)
Choisya (Mexican orange blossom)
Fagus (Beech)
Eucalyptus (Gum)
Fatsia (Japanese fatsia)
Ferns (various)
Gaultheria shallon (Salal, Shallon)
Hedera (Ivy)

Hydrangea macrophylla (Hydrangea)
Liquidambar (Sweetgum)
Moluccella laevis (Bells of Ireland)
Prunus sargentii (Sargent cherry)
Quercus robur (Common oak)
Quercus ilex (Holm oak)
Selaginella kraussiana (Spikemoss)
Senecio 'Sunshine' (Senecio)

Stand stems in a glycerine solution

PRESERVING PLANTS WITH DESICCANTS

A number of desiccants (drying agents) can be used to dry flowers that are not too fleshy petalled or stemmed. The best results are obtained with silica gel, but this must be handled with great care, using a mask and rubber gloves. Dried borax or alum with silver sand will also coax the moisture out of flowers and leaves, but the process is slower than with silica gel.

Good Plants for Desiccants

Alstroemeria (Peruvian lily)
Convallaria (Lily-of-the-valley)
Dahlia (Dahlia)
Eustoma (Lisianthius)
Freesia (Freesia)
Gerbera (Gerbera)
Gladiolus (Gladiolus)

Lilium (Lily)
Narcissus (Daffodil)
Paeonia (Peony)
Ranunculus (Buttercup)
Rosa (Rose)
Tulipa (Tulip)
Zinnia (Zinnia)

USING SILICA GEL
Buy silica gel as very fine crystals. Dry the gel by putting it in a low oven for several hours. Place a thin layer of gel in an airtight box. Lay the flowers on top and add more gel to submerge the flowers. Put on the lid and leave for two days, then check: the flowers will crumble if overdried.

PRESERVING PLANTS WITH BORAX AND ALUM
Mix three parts of either borax or alum with two parts silver sand. Ensure that the mixture is dry (but not hot) before use by placing in a low oven for several hours. Follow the same procedure as for silica gel, but wait at least ten days before checking whether the plant material is dry.

STEAMING FLOWERS

Revive dried flowers that are squashed or crumpled by holding them in the steam from a boiling kettle. The petals will start to flop down with moisture within minutes. When this movement begins, hold the flowers away from the steam and upside down. Blow gently up into the petals to separate them out. Keep blowing until the petals are set in their new, refreshed shape.

Flagging petals are revived

STORING DRIED FLOWERS

The cardboard boxes that flowers are sold in at markets are ideal for storing dried flowers, and these should be obtainable from your local florist. Layer bunches of flowers into the boxes, supporting the flower stems just below their heads with crumpled tissue or kitchen paper. Make sure that the flowers are not crushed or overcrowded, as they are quite brittle when dry. Replace the lids and store the boxes in a cool, dry place.

SUGARING FLOWERS

Edible sugared flowers are very simple to make and provide delightful cake decorations that will keep for up to three days. The prettiest flowers to use are violets, roses, and primroses; tuberous begonia flower petals can also be prepared in this way. As the process uses raw egg white, these sugared flowers should not be eaten by pregnant women or elderly people.

As a cake decoration, arrange petals to resemble flowers

1 LIGHTLY BEAT an egg white in a small bowl until the egg is broken down but not frothy. With a fine paintbrush, coat the petals on both sides with the beaten egg white.

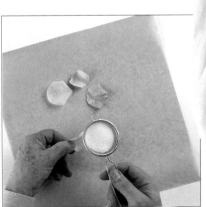

2 USING A STRAINER, sprinkle the petals with granulated sugar. Place gently on a fine mesh cake rack or waxed paper and leave in a warm, dry place until dry.

WIRING PLANT MATERIAL

I try to use wired flowers as little as possible, preferring to use each stem of flower and foliage for its own natural attributes. However, if your selection is limited, wiring can strengthen damaged or bent stems and make them usable. For wreaths and swags, on the other hand, wiring is often the only way to achieve the shape you want. The very stiff stems of dried flowers can also benefit from wiring, either to slightly bend a hollow stem or to group bunches to put into an arrangement.

WIRING FRESH FLOWERS

Fresh flowers can be wired in a number of ways for use in wedding bouquets, swags, or garlands. The key point is to use wires that support the flowers without adding too much extra weight: wired bouquets can become very heavy, so the lighter the flower, the finer the stub wire you should use (see p.172). Stub wires can be covered with a green or brown rubber tape so that they resemble flower stems and blend into the arrangement. It is often possible to strengthen a stem by simply sticking a stub wire into the stem just below the flower head, but if you want to ensure that a flower is securely wired, thread a fine silver rose wire through the stems, then wind it around both stem and supporting stub wire. This method can also be used on flowers with very fine stems.

1 CUT OFF THE STEM 2.5cm (1in) below the flower head. Hold a stub wire against the stem, with the tip just touching the flower head. Run fine rose wire from the stem end to just under the flower head.

2 START BINDING the silver rose wire around the stub wire and stem, binding in the short end of the rose wire to secure it. Continue binding down the stem and stub wire for about 7.5cm (3in) then cut the wire.

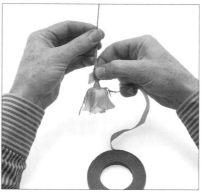

3 HOLD THE WIRED flower head upside down. Place the end of the binding tape against the stem, close to the flower head. Wind the tape tightly around the stem by rotating the stub wire between your finger and thumb.

4 CONTINUE TO WIND the binding tape firmly around the stub wire until the entire wire has been covered. Twist the tape tightly at the end so that it adheres to itself. Cut off the remaining tape.

HOLLOW AND SOFT STEMS

Wire flowers with short soft stems, such as those used in wedding work, by pushing a wire up through the stem into the flower. Flowers with hollow stems can also be wired easily this way. With larger hollow-stemmed flowers, such as amaryllis and arum lily, it is best to wire individual flowers as described in the step-by-step instructions on the opposite page.

Push thin stub wire into cut-off narrow, hollow stem

NARROW STEMS

Push the stub wire up the narrow, hollow stem as far as it will go. Secure it by piercing the stem with rose wire just under the flower head and binding the fine wire down around the stem and the stub wire.

WIRING BUNCHES

FRESH MATERIAL

When you are making up garlands, swags, or wedding bouquets that require wired, fresh plant material, it speeds up the work process considerably if you wire small bunches of flowers or flowers and foliage together. After stem-taping the wire, the bunch can then be inserted as required. This is particularly useful when mixing delicate small flower heads with feathery foliage for wedding bouquets.

1 PREPARE THE plant material first by removing some of the lower leaves. Place the stub wire at an angle across the stem about 4cm (1½in) above the cut end, and leaving about 6cm (2½in) of wire free at the top.

2 STARTING JUST below the flower head, wind the free end of the stub wire around the stem and around the stub wire itself so the stem is secured. Continue binding the stub wire down the stem, finishing just below its cut end.

DRIED FLOWERS

The process of wiring dried flowers is very similar to that of wiring fresh flowers (*see above*). By using wire, you can manage good-sized bunches of dried flowers – perhaps to be incorporated into large dried arrangements. The bunches can consist of the same flowers, or a mixture, depending on your design.

2 HOLD A PIECE of stub wire that is stout enough to support the whole bunch of material against the flower or plant stems – about 2.5cm (1in) up from the stem bases. Twist the wire tightly around the bunch and over itself, leaving a long and a short end of wire.

3 PLACE THE LONG end of stub wire against the stems. Twist the short end of wire down and around the bunch, including the long end of wire. Be sure to keep the short end of wire taut so that it holds the bunch of dried flowers firmly.

1 FIRST ASSEMBLE the individual pieces of dried plant material you want to use in your arrangement, choosing undamaged or freshly steamed specimens.

WIRING CONES AND FRUITS

Most plant material is straightforward to wire in the ways already described. Fir cones (which I like to use in autumn and winter arrangements) and fruits require a different approach, however. Many fruits can be wired by pushing a stub wire through from the stalk end; when it comes through the other end, bend the top into a short U shape and draw the wire back through the fruit. This works well with small citrus fruits, apples, and crab apples. Wiring a fir cone is described below.

Sweet chestnut

Fir cone

Red apple

1 PASS A PIECE OF STUB WIRE of a suitable weight to bear the fir cone across the stalk end of the cone, just where it starts to curve in. Wedge the wire into the first band of woody scales, leaving 5cm (2in) jutting out.

2 WIND THE STUB WIRE around the fir cone, pulling it in towards the centre, underneath the woody scales. Continue winding the wire around, under the scales, until the short and long ends overlap.

3 TWIST THE TWO ENDS OF WIRE together for several turns, then pull the long end of the wire down under the cone so that it appears to emerge from the base of the cone. Snip off the short end of the wire.

USING WIRE HAIRPINS

Made from sections of stub wire, U-shaped "hairpins" are useful for attaching moss or other covering materials to chicken-wire frames, to florist's foam, or for holding pieces of plant material in position on frames or bases. They are also invaluable when creating swags or wreaths. As with all wiring techniques, choose the lightest possible wires to do the job efficiently.

Moss pinned around candle base

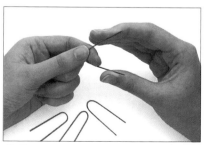

1 CUT LENGTHS OF STUB WIRE so that they are long enough to push deeply into the frame once they are bent into a U shape or, for heavier attachments, will go through the frame with enough length to be bent back.

2 LAY PIECES of covering material, such as moss, against the frame and pin them in with the hairpins. Attach single plant or flower stems to frames or bases with two hairpins.

WIRING FOR SHAPE

Although it is always best to choose flowers and foliage for their natural shapes, it can sometimes be useful to give very straight stems more character by wiring them into different shapes. Bear in mind, however, that only the gentlest curves look convincing. If the stem will not be seen, simply twist a stub wire or mossing wire in a spiral down its length and then gently bend it into a curve.

HOLLOW STEMS

Flowers with hollow stems, such as antirrhinums and larkspur, simply require a stub wire pushed up the stem as far as it will go. You can then gently ease the stem into a natural-looking curve to suit your arrangement.

A wired, hollow stem can be bent into a gentle curve

REPAIRING STEMS

Repair a broken stem by inserting a length of stub wire into each end of the break and pushing the pieces together. For the flower to survive, however, the broken stem must be below water level so that the flower can continue to take up water.

Repair a broken stem with a wire reinforcement

GLUEING MATERIAL

A glue gun is useful when creating dried flower arrangements, though it can also be used for attaching fresh flowers – to twigs or sapling branches, for example. There are two types of glue gun: they look the same, but one type operates at a high temperature and gives a very firm bond; the other works with a cooler melting glue and is therefore safer to use, although the bond is not as secure.

USING A GLUE GUN

Pre-heat the glue gun. Clean the surfaces to be glued, then apply a small amount of glue to each surface. Hold the surfaces together for about one minute until the glue has set.

Attach plant material with glue gun

INDEX

A

B

C

ACKNOWLEDGMENTS

AUTHOR'S ACKNOWLEDGMENTS

I would like to thank the following for their help in creating the original *Flowers*: photographer Stephen Hayward, with assistant Paul Lund, for his stunning images, infinite patience, and for never being daunted by a studio floor that was constantly awash with flowers. Not to mention the Dunsfold village store for a constant supply of doughnuts.

The team from Dorling Kindersley who were wonderful to work with: editors Lesley Malkin (carrying baby Finlay) and Irene Lyford, and art editor Wendy Bartlet. Dennis Edwards, Lee Ward, and David Donovan at John Austin; David Hancock, Ian Potter, and Tony Flavin at Baker and Duguid; and David Bacon at A & F Bacon – all at New Covent Garden Market, London, who helped me search out most of the plant material for the book. Also Terracottas of New Covent Garden for many pots; Stephen Camburn of Gaudiamus, New Kings Road, London, for lending some of his stunning terracotta containers; Babylon Design, Fulham Road, London.

A special thank you to Dr C. Andrew Henley, who travelled to various locations in Australia to photograph plants for us; and to the following people who helped him: Albert's Garden, Pialligo, ACT; Marcus Harvey, Hillview Rare Plants, Hobart, Tas; Dean Havelberg, Hillview, Exeter, NSW; Marcia Voce, Birchfield Herbs, Bungendore, NSW; Dirk Wallace, Wodonga, Vic.

Lastly, and most importantly, I would like to thank Rodney Engen for all his help and tremendous inspirational input.

PUBLISHER'S ACKNOWLEDGMENTS

Dorling Kindersley would like to thank Sue Barraclough, Joanna Chisholm, Jane Cooke, Candida Frith-MacDonald, Jenny Jones, Jane Laing, Kathryn Lane, Frank Ritter, and Susannah Steel for invaluable editorial assistance; Fiona Wild and Henrietta Llewellyn-Davis for punctilious proofreading; and Michelle Clark for compiling the index. Alison Lotinga, Alison Shackleton, and Ann Thompson for design assistance; Wesley Richards for design assistance and artwork on the flower symbols. Amanda Russell for painstaking picture research. Mark Bracey and Robert Campbell for DTP support.

COMMISSIONED PHOTOGRAPHY

All photographs by Stephen Hayward except:
Andreas Einsiedel 172–173, 182–183, 184–185, 186–187; Dr C. Andrew Henley; Dave King 172–173, 178–179, 182–183, 184–185, 186–187; Diana Miller 182–183, 186–187; Matthew Ward 174–175, 180–181.